Historic Glimpses of
Trees of the West

Historic Glimpses of
Trees of the West

A Journey with Lambert Florin

Huge copper beech, *(opposite) Fagus silvatica,* grows on campus of Reed College in Portland, Oregon. Close relative, *F. americana,* is native to eastern states. Although tree has large, convoluted bole, bark is unusually smooth. It is said this is why Daniel Boone used it for his frequent carved autographs (without the "e").

Superior PUBLISHING COMPANY

SEATTLE, WASHINGTON

Library of Congress Card Number 76-28982

Library of Congress Cataloging in Publication Data

Florin, Lambert.
Historic Glimpses of Trees of the West.

Includes index.
1. The West—History—Pictorial works.

2. Historic trees—The West—Pictorial works.
I. Title. II. Title: Trees of the West.
F591.F5745   978   76-28982
ISBM 0-87564-339-6

FIRST EDITION

PRINTED IN THE UNITED STATES OF AMERICA

This book is dedicated to the memory of Myrtle McGuire
who patiently handed me the tripod, light meter and filter.

Contents

*All photographs and sketches in this book
unless otherwise credited are the work of
Lambert Florin*

PREFACE

What is there about a tree that holds our attention, fascinates us, draws us close to study design of leaf and bark and ventures the remark . . . "Well, I think that's some kind of ash."

Well, a tree has signs all over it to tell us it's a living thing, a truly wonderful mechanism of nature. Its germination from a seed and its growth to maturity are rather like our own and it is far more self-sufficient than the most independent of men. With all those branches and leaves it catches all the sunshine it needs. Its roots draw plenty of nourishment from the soil and it stands there in defiance of the ill winds of fortune so that you can pick its blossoms and fruit or if ruthless, cut it down for furniture or firewood. It will also just keep on growing so you can say to your grandchildren . . . "I planted that apple tree long before you were born, and I'll bet it will still be there when you're as old as I am and you can say to your grandchildren . . . "

So trees are very close to all of us whether we realize it or not and while this book explores western trees in some detail and does contain some technical terms, it is clearly not a botanical key. There are many such reference books essential to identification which add greatly to the enjoyment of the arboreal kingdom. Some treat all plants, some are confined to trees along with others giving thorough study to certain classes of trees . . . such as *The Genus Pinus* by N.T. Mirov.

Another point. This book does not encompass all western trees or even all western trees in single categories. So the question is, what is Florin trying to do to us? Well, he has for many years traveled the western mountains and deserts in search of such things as ghost towns, remnants of old horse-drawn vehicles, historic churches, forgotten weed-grown cemeteries and wooden headboards rotting in them . . . yes, even the once essential outdoor privy. These subjects and many more have been featured in books my publisher terms "photo histories". At the same time the author, a plantsman since childhood, has always been well aware of the trees growing near the pioneer wagon, the elaborately carved marble tombstone or the ones shading the weather-beaten little john.

LAMBERT FLORIN

Pow Wow Tree is big leaf maple or Oregon maple or broadleaf maple or white maple—*Acer macrophyllum.* Historic specimen still growing on north bank of Clackamas River at Gladstone, Oregon, has several times approached destruction from natural forces and man himself. Amputation of huge upper limbs has reduced height to 40', spread to 25'. C. Ralph Vooris of state forestry department estimates one time height as 80' to 90'. Champion big leaf maple, he says, is one in Valsetz area, 96' high with spread of 94'. Pow Wow Tree in summer appears healthy with still burgeoning foliage, in winter presents sad spectacle of senility.

The
POW WOW
tree

Battered and scarred, witness to Indian raids and rites, and to the tribe's final retirement into the shadows, the Pow Wow maple of the Clackamas still stands sentinel to the profound stability of the pioneer spirit.

In the 16th Anniversary Edition of the Gladstone (Oregon) *Morning Enterprise,* writer Oscar Freytag relates the colorful history of the famous tree. His account is given here in part.

"Sixty years ago the birth of the Morning Enterprise marked the establishment and recognition of a new order of things in a country just emerging from primeval state.

Lying for centuries untold, awaiting the coming of a race who would, by industry and for gainful purposes, bring about changes that would sometimes beautify, sometimes mar, the landmark of the creator; a people who would evolve a civilization then undreamed of in this unpromising wilderness, who would transform the forests into fruitful farms and beautiful cities and into a countryside later to become the playground of the nation.

In the early days prior to the coming of the white man, the Indian who inhabited the region of the northwest, roamed much as his pale faced successor is now doing, with less ease and comfort to be sure, but doubtless as happily according to his rights.

A gathering place for these early inhabitants for ceremonials and feasts of rejoining was the giant maple tree that has stood for more years than man can tell on the banks of the beautiful Clackamas river not far from where its waters join those of the Willamette river. Under the spreading branches of this tree pow-wows were held, and it is today known far and wide as the "Pow-Wow Maple". The various tribes of the northwest assembled here, coming in the fair days of June when the spring freshet in the Columbia river backed up the waters of the Willamette, its usual swift current like a placid lake, and making the voyage of the Indians less difficult and dangerous.

Gaily bedecked in beaded trappings, great headdresses of feathers, and painted in weird and fanciful fashion, the Indians must have presented a gorgeous sight as they paddled their long canoes up the river to the appointed rendezvous at the old maple tree. Here they gathered and held their conferences with a loud beating of the tom toms, dancing and howling, with great pomp and ceremony conducting their pow-wows.

In the season when the salmon were running and when the deer and other game were prime, bands of Indians came to the banks of the Clackamas which was a veritable storehouse from which they would draw their supplies for the year. Salmon fishing was not the sport of the present day when runs are small and fish temperamental, and only to be caught when their mood is right. In those early days the salmon were so plentiful that when a run was in full tide, it was necessary in order to ford the river for some one to lead the way for the traveler, beating the fish to one side with clubs, to form a passage way. The Indian, knowing no law but that of appropriation, took the fish by easy means, using only the choicest portions for their fare. Preservation, by drying and smoking, was the Indians mode of making salmon last until the fish appeared for spawning the following year.

Forests in those days, were kept clear of underbrush by the Indians, thus minimizing the danger of forest fires and rendering their hunting of game less difficult. Many darts and arrow heads have been found in the fields that have taken the place of the forests, and near the maple tree are mute evidences of the hunting that the Indians enjoyed.

Roots, such as wapatoes, camas, white fern roots, and other vegetation, were plentiful and all these foods were to be had for the taking, making visits of the Indians in large numbers of frequent occurrence. During these pilgrimages in quest of food, many scenes of festivities were enacted under the maple tree and later, battles were fought. The Clackamas tribe which made their home near the old tree were ignorant and lowly, but peaceable and friendly, as they went about lazily garnering their stores, the jealous and warlike Molallas would descend upon them, and wage a war which they hoped would be productive of stores of food. The braves, whose families by that time were living by the generosity of Peter M. Rinearson on land he had taken up in 1846 as a donation land claim, would send the squaws and children to the Rinearson home, where they were hidden by Mrs. Rinearson in a large closet under the broad, winding stairway until the Molallas had been vanquished, and sent back to their haunts some miles to the South East. Sometimes before leaving the Molallas would tramp around the large home of the Rinearsons, peering in the windows, but later a wholesome fear of Mr. Rinearson and respect for his prowess kept the Indians in check.

Clackamas George, the chief of the Clackamas tribe, living in one of the rude houses on the Rinearson land, went to the big house one day after imbibing too freely of fire water, not unlike that of the white man's, caused him to be boisterous and threatening, and with one blow of his leaded cane carried always by him for protection against wandering Indians, Mr. Rinearson felled the unruly chief. Ever after this episode Mr. Rinearson was held in high esteem by all the Indians for his temerity in striking and subduing that exalted personage—a chief— and Indian George called the following day to make amends to this man of courage. Mr. Rinearson, known to the Indians as Mr. Peter, was good to the Indians, and when they wished to know what the white sahla tyee in Washington wanted to tell them, they took papers to Mr. Peter, who would give them the message.

The home of the Indian until the coming of the white man had been the usual teepee, but later they built crude houses, perhaps 15 by 18 in dimension, made of battered boards of all sizes and shapes, picked up as they could be found, and roofed with shakes. In a dugout in the center of the one room the fire was built, the smoke going out through a small opening in the roof. The entire family lived and all the functions of domestic life were carried on in this room, and visiting Indians were likewise made at home in these small quarters.

E.C. Hackett of Oregon City, county recorder, was born up the Clackamas River on the land now owned and occupied by Dr. Coffey of Portland, and remembers three Indian chiefs who were identified with activities centering around the Pow-Wow maple. These chiefs were Wacheno, Clackamas Jake, and Clackamas George. The Indian names of the last two named chiefs are not known.

Clackamas River is placid in autumn, at least in lower stretches, while upper stream is mountain torrent, especially in spring freshets. Confluence with Willamette is few hundred feet west, left, out of photo. State Highway 99 E crosses on bridge in foreground, nearing Oregon City. Pow Wow Tree is located on opposite bank near RR bridge in background. Cottonwood trees in right foreground are typical of these river loving members of poplar tribe. One common name is balsam poplar in reference to sweet perfume exhaled in spring as large resin coated leaf buds expand.

Plaque was presented and placed in 1937 by Camp Fire Girls who raised money with many and varied projects. In accordance with natural effort to heal wounds, venerable tree is gradually covering marker. First Oregon State Fair in 1861 was able to place most of exhibits under or near then hugely spreading branches, with trunk itself serving as corner fence post.

East facing side of time worn Pow Wow Tree shows ravages, main trunk rotted and finally amputated in major surgery. Side trunk, more solid and vigorous, is itself truncated at height of 40'. Among other adversities, tree faced complete destruction when street improvement threatened removal. Public outcry forced compromise and road now swings around eroded trunk, west-bound traffic warned of obstacle by reflector marker.

Richard Greaves of Oregon City, a stepson of Peter Rinearson, and reared from early boyhood on the Rinearson donation land claim, also recalls witnessing some of the ceremonies. An Indian wedding taking place under the maple tree was attended by Mr. Hackett and Mr. Greaves. The happy groom, John Dick, came from his Washougal home to court Nancy, the daughter of Maria, bringing with him seven ponies as a gift to the old chief. The chief was not pleased with John Dick's offering, and sent him back for seven more ponies. Returning with the required number of ponies, John obtained the consent of the old chief, and the betrothal and marriage ceremonies were allowed to proceed. Much food was consumed, and with noise and dancing, the Indians performed the betrothal rites, the women of the tribe wearing bright calico dresses, many strings of beads, and the inevitable shawls.

An old squaw, supposed to be possessed of psychic powers, performed the feather ceremony which was presumed to drive away the evil spirits, leaving the young couple in peace. This old squaw, throwing feathers into the air with a peculiar gurgling cry, and dipping and rising in a rhythmic dance, would blow feathers, circling around the tree at some distance, and blowing the feathers away from the ceremonial spot and the high contracting parties. This rite was repeated for three evenings, dancing and rejoicing going on all the while. The marriage ceremony was simple and was quickly performed. The bride Nancy was carried from her home nearby on the back of a squaw, covered from head to foot with a blanket. She was set down by the squaw on a small hummock under the pow wow tree, closely covered by the blanket. John Dick, was carried on the back of a brave, was placed beside his bride, the blanket thrown on both, and they were pronounced man and wife.

On the east side of the track of the P.E.P. Co., lies the site of the Indian burial ground. A part of this tract is now traversed by Clackamas Boulevard and Arlington street, and excavations for street improvements and for homes which now occupy this land, have unearthed many trinkets traded to the Indians by the Hudson's Bay company, such as huge brass keys, rings and bracelets, and many beads of various sizes, which had been buried with the Indians. Skeletons have been exposed, and on one occasion the writer found a perfect skull of a Flathead Indian, which was sent to the Smithsonian Institute, where it was gratefully received and placed in the museum.

A part of the tract was used by Indians who did not wish to enter the bodies of their departed relatives, but who placed them on boards secured horizontally in the trees and here they rested in peace. These Indians also were no doubt provided with the usual trinkets for the use in the Happy Hunting grounds. The old maple tree, however is now associated in the minds of those who recall the scenes under its shelter with sadness or death, only scenes of joy and mirth seem to have been carried on there.

The tree, old and gnarled, stands on the north side of the country road, now known as Clackamas boulevard, which skirts the Clackamas River, and is little more than a block west of the tracks of the Portland Electric Power company in the city of Gladstone, and is possibly one of the last trees that stood in this vicinity when the white man came, and it is rich in tradition and historical value. It is the wish of many who are interested in retaining the few remaining land marks of the days that are gone, that some steps be taken which will insure the preservation of this grand old tree, that the community, not Gladstone nor Clackamas county alone, but the entire state, may point to it as one of the spots which figured large in the early history of the Oregon country. It is hoped that the tree may be surrounded with a protecting fence, and that a suitable marker be placed thereon. Travelers from all over the world passing by under the welcome shade of the old maple tree will find an especial interest in knowing that this tree marks one of the historical spots of the northwest."

And the Pow Wow Tree was marked as an historical site in 1937. The Oregon City *Banner-Courier* covered the ceremonial event in its issue of May 7 of that year.

"With perhaps a half dozen men lynched on it," the article stated, "and many Indian pow wows held under it, the glorious old maple tree on the river road in Gladstone has come into public recognition for the first time.

"At the annual Campfire dinner held by the Gladstone campfire girls Monday night a motion was passed to give the old tree its long hidden glory. This tree, which must be several hundred years old, also marked the entry way to the first Oregon State Fair held in Gladstone.

"A discussion was held at the meeting for the purpose of bringing some of the glory to Gladstone that it deserves as being one of the oldest settlements in this part of the country. The general plan is to make a sort of celebration to honor the tree and to perform some badly needed tree-surgery on it. A marker is to be purchased and put on the tree to tell the history of the old landmark, and a program of pagentry is planned."

Yet there was trouble to come. The Portland Oregon *Journal* and local newspapers quoted the county agent as predicting disaster for the famous old tree unless something could be done to save it. The *Journal* article went on to say,

"A huge old maple tree—its age unknown—bids fair to become object of controversy out in Gladstone and anywhere else tree-lovers and history-lovers exist. It might get cut down.

"It is called the Pow Wow tree, because of its use as a landmark to Indians over a century ago who supposedly held a number of powwows at its base. It was site of the first Oregon state fair in 1861. The tree stands close to the Clackamas river, about a mile east of the Pacific highway on the north shore of the river.

"Clackamas boulevard, which roughly parallels the river, makes a deep bend at the site of the tree so as to miss it.

"The old tree, originally forked, has only one full fork left. The streetside fork, part of which came down in a storm a number of years ago, is succumbing to disease and old age. A huge cavity on the south side is big enough to put a person in. Because of the old age of the big tree and weakening of its base, Clackamas county horticultural agents have suggested that the tree be cut down as a hazard.

"Members of the Gladstone chamber of commerce, however, according to its president, Merle Brown, don't want that to happen. They have put out an appeal for other agencies to help.

"It has been suggested that possibly careful trimming of the top of the tree, together with a sealing up of the rotten spot, might keep it going for a few more years.

"About 1936, before part of one fork was blown down, a group of Camp Fire girls in Gladstone collected some money to have the Pow Wow tree fixed up a little. At that time cement was put into the then smaller rotten space.

"Mrs. M.E. Turner of Gladstone, who was leader of the group then, reports that it was some years after this that the big section was blown down in a storm. She also said that the Camp Fire girls paid for the installation of the second bronze plaque in the tree's base. This plaque, labelled "Indian Pow Wow Tree, Entrance to First State Fair, 1861," is on the south side.

"Partly overgrown by the trunk is an earlier plaque on the street side which says the same thing. Brown said a chamber of commerce committee has been named to consult with tree surgeons for advice on what can be done to save the old landmark."

The tree surgeon's operation was a success—and the patient lived.

DAWN REDWOODS
have ancient lineage

__Metasequoia,__ nurtured in Portland, Oregon has
"family tree" going back 100 million years in China.

"A race of ancestral redwood trees which flourished 100,000,000 years ago is surviving in a remote valley deep in the interior of China.

"These trees are known as the dawn redwoods—themselves between five and six centuries old, and prototypes of the strain. Their race is older than the human race, older than the mastodons and the pigmy horses, as old as the giant dinosaurs. They represent the incredibly ancient forerunners of the modern redwoods now growing in California and Oregon.

"With the prehistoric animals, dawn redwoods had supposedly become extinct about 20,000,000 years ago, leaving behind only the fossil traces of their distinctive needles and cones.

"Three of these "living fossils," however, were seen alive by Dr. Ralph Chaney of the University of California and the Carnegie Institute of Washington.

"'To me,' he said, 'finding a living dawn redwood is at least as remarkable as discovering a living dinosaur.'

"He confirmed the fact of their existence—an unparalleled epic of survival—after traveling more than 10,000 miles by airplane from San Francisco to Chungking and then by river boat down the Yangtze Kiang. The last stage of his journey, from the little town of Wanhsien, took three days over muddy, slippery trails which zigzagged over a succession of mile-high mountain ranges.

"Although groups of bandits were reported operating around these mountain trails and robbing travelers, none came any closer than 100 feet of the party.

"There is no doubt that members of the dawn redwood race have really survived. We have seen them, touched them, photographed them, measured them and examined their green buds. We have even climbed them.

This article by Milton Silverman was copyrighted 1949 by
North American Newspaper Alliance,
Chronicle Publishing Co.

Ardent plantsman John Bacher of early Swiss Floral in Portland, Oregon, was among first eager recipients of Dawn Redwood, *Metasequoa*, seeds when sent out by Arnold Arboretum Harvard University, Boston, Mass. in 1948. Always successful with germination of seeds, Bacher grew a number of the little trees which he distributed to botanical gardens. One was planted in Portland's Rhododendron Test Gardens, haven for many species of rare shrubs and trees. Now sturdy and well established, this Dawn Redwood grows at edge one of many waterways in gardens.

"Their trunks are like modern redwoods, big and ribbed and buttressed at the base. Their bark is like modern redwood bark, although considerably thinner and smoother. Their branches, beginning nearly at the base of the trees, extend outward and upward.

"The most striking difference lies in the foliage. Modern redwoods, like most cone-bearing trees, are evergreen and carry their leaves or needles all year long. But the dawn redwood, although a conifer, is not evergreen; it loses its needles in winter.

"All three of the dawn redwoods we first saw are growing close together on a rice-paddy bank only a few hundred yards from the Ho-tao-chi, the village of Grindstone River. Two of them are small, young trees. The third is relatively gigantic—10 feet, 10 inches in diameter at the base and 98 feet high.

"On the basis of test borings and ring counts, Dr. Chaney estimates the age of this big dawn redwood at between five and six centuries.

"'This tree was born at least a century before Columbus discovered America,' he declared. 'It was a tall tree when the Ming dynasty ruled China, and it was old when the Manchu emperors came into power.'

"Towering over this mountain-guarded valley, the big tree is revered by the villagers as the abode of a god. "There must be a god in the tree," explained 60-year-old Cheng Yu-men. "It is the biggest, strongest, straightest tree for many days of travel, bigger than any other we have ever seen."

"Sixteen years ago, he and several other village elders built a little mud-and-tile temple right at the base of the tree. A village official asserted that a brew made from fragments of the bark, plus prayers to the tree god, had saved the life of his dying daughter.

REPTILE AGE:

**Dawn Redwoods Recall
Crolaceous Period.**

"Fossil remains of the dawn redwoods—now known technically as Metasequoia—were first found in 1828 in rocks near Frankfort, Germany. Scientists have long believed this genus of prehistoric life had vanished, since no living dawn redwoods had ever been reported from any continent by scientific explorers.

"In 1945, however, there appeared the first hints that perhaps this ancient race might possibly have survived. From the little-known border country between Szechwan and Hupeh provinces, three young Chinese plant collectors brought out some puzzling specimens—needles, cones and seeds—which did not seem to belong to any known tree.

"These specimens were sent to Dr. W.C. Cheng of the National Central university at Nanking and to Dr. H.H. Hu, director of the Fan Memorial institute at Peiping. Both agreed the specimens bore an amazing resemblance to the fossilized needles and cones of the dawn redwoods. In a joint report, they announced their decision in a Chinese technical journal.

"They also sent some specimens to America—to Dr. Elmer Drew Merrill at Harvard, who also wrote a brief technical report, and to Dr. Chaney at the University of California.

"Confirmation seemed essential. No trained observer had seen the trees. The whole thing might be a mistake, or some kind of incomprehensible hoax.

"We reached Wah-hsien by flying from Shanghai over rugged, snow-capped mountains to Chungking. From Chungking, wartime capital of China, we came by sampan and river boat to Wan-hsien. With us were Wilon Chen, our interpreter, and C.T. Hwa, one of the plant collectors who had himself visited the area last year.

"There is no road from Wan-hsien to Ho-tao-chi. Neither jeep, nor horse, nor even rickshaw can get through the mountain trail. So we hired seven coolies to carry our baggage—heavy winter clothes, sleeping bags, medical supplies, scientific equipment, army K rations and a few cans of food for an emergency—and a dozen men to carry us in sedan chairs.

"On the second day, after learning bandits were in the area, we acquired an escort of soldiers—a few ragged, straw-sandaled youths equipped with antique carbines—who cost us $60,000 (Chinese) a day apiece, about 18 cents in U.S. money.

"Again we followed a trail through the canyons, up and down—mostly up—and at night, after chalking up 27 miles, we reached Lung-chu-pa, the village of the excellent horse. Next afternoon, we went right up a 60-degree shoulder of a mountain, crossed a pass at 4750 feet, and descended into the valley of Mo-tao-chi. Our mileage for the day—28.

"When we went out to see the dawn redwoods, we were accompanied by nearly everyone in town. While Dr. Chaney made his measurements and took his photographs, untold numbers of chickens and pigs were trodden underfoot, one of our soldiers slammed his own shins with his own gun, and four children and one adult slipped into the not altogether clean water of an adjacent rice paddy. The people hadn't had such a good time, the magistrate told us later, since the local tax collectors had fallen into their own cesspool.

"The three dawn redwoods of Mo-tao-chi, growing in the unnatural environment on the banks of a rice paddy, were only a sample of what was to come. Hearing reports of many dawn redwoods to the south, Dr. Chaney and the rest of us started next for Wang-shia-ying in Hupeh province. The travel was difficult, especially on the short-cut we decided to take.

"But the journey's end was worth the hardship for there we found a lost world—a world that existed more than a million centuries ago. It is a mysteriously protected segment of the earth as it appeared during the age of reptiles, when gigantic dinosaurs and flying saurians were lords of all creation. Here, on this red sandy soil, once lived the horn-headed dinosaur and the terrifying flesh-eating tyrannosaur. Here are the trees—ancient species of oak, sassafras, birch, sweet gum, laurel and katsura—which sheltered the brontosaur, the enormous vegetarian.

The Dawn Redwood, *(opposite top)* *Metasequoia*, differs greatly from its modern relatives, the coastal redwood and related giant sequoia of the Sierra. It drops its needles for winter. Bill Robinson of Portland Park Bureau was anxious to propagate more of the plants than those few originating from first seeds sent from China in the '40s. Experimenting, he found cuttings taken from the young seedlings grew readily and rapidly. This fair-sized tree, photographed in January, was grown in that fashion. It is located with several others for company near horseshoe pitching area of Laurelhurst Park, Portland, Oregon.

Hoyt Arboretum of Portland, Oregon, *(opposite bottom)* displays many exotic trees from all parts of world. None has a more fascinating history than the Dawn Redwood, this one established later than one at Rhododendron Test Gardens. Growing in small open meadow, this tree conveniently offered its foliage for close up photograph. Where other redwoods have rough, rasping leaves the Dawn Redwood's are soft to touch. Another striking difference is the shedding of its leaves in fall, appearing as naked as any maple or elm.

"And here, by the hundreds, are the dawn redwoods—the ancient race of trees which were kings of the forest a hundred million years ago, just as the dinosaurs were kings of the animal world. It is definitely not a land of make-believe. It really exists. The mountains of seven humps, Tha-chi-yao-shan, have been surveyed by American airmen who give a peak elevation of 7175 feet. The valley of dawn redwoods lies roughly at 30 degrees 9 minutes north, and 108 degrees 37 minutes east, just east of the Szechuan-Hupeh border.

"'We have come a hundred miles by trail and a hundred million years in history,' said Dr. Chaney. 'Now, for the first time, we can see with our own eyes how the world really looked in Cretaceous times, in the age of reptiles.'

Dr. Chaney was the first white man to reach this village. He confirmed the existence of more than 100 dawn redwoods within a few miles of Shui-hsa-pa. Some of them are growing along rice paddies in this narrow winding valley. Others are in steep canyons leading off to the sides. Many of them are from 60 to 90 feet high. In these canyon areas, the dawn redwoods are growing not in groves as the modern redwoods do in California and Oregon, but in mixed forests. Their neighbors are ancient species of oak, sassafras, sweet gum or liquid amber, and particularly cercidiphyllum or katsura.

"'This is just like running into a botanical alumni - reunion,' Dr. Chaney declared. 'Nowhere else in the world do these trees grow together naturally. The only place they are found as neighbors is in fossil records—in rock deposits dating back 100,000,000 to 120,000,000 years, the period when dinosaurs were roaming the earth.'

LUCKY TREE:
Residents of Valley
Claim Bountiful Crops

"He claimed the canyons here seemed so typical of a 'dinosaur landscape' that the sudden appearance of a flesh-eating tyrant-dinosaur, roaring up one of these canyons, would be quite appropriate.

"No such appearance occurred. Unquestionably, dinosaurs existed in his region of China and very possibly stalked through this very valley. Only a few miles away, in the so-called 'Red Basin of Szechuan,' scientists have found fossilized bones of the ancient reptiles.

"The villagers here have a vague idea there is something remarkable about these trees. They say the dawn redwood is a lucky tree, a tree to be respected. They think it is some kind of pine that needs much water, and call it Thui-shui-hsa, or 'water pine.' The name of their village means place of the water pine.

"The first inhabitants came here about 300 years ago. Now the population has soared to about 70 men, women and children, all living in five big houses. These are like other village houses in this part of China—dirty, cold, reeking with nauseous vapors, populated by rats, fleas, cockroaches, lice, chickens, pigs, dogs and children sorely in need of handkerchiefs. Every floor is encrusted with more than a century's accumulation of human and animal filth.

"But this valley is something else. When you get beyond sight—and smell—of the village, the fields and paddies are lush and rich and clean. The mountains on both sides are covered with forests, not curved and hacked like other Chinese mountains to give room for just one more bunch of rice or one more mound of corn.

"'Every year we have more rice and corn and cabbage and wheat and beans than we can eat,' claims Wu Tsa Ming, the head man of the village. 'Our trees give us plums, peaches, pears, walnuts, chestnuts, apples and cherries. We have many pigs and chickens and cows, and strong horses and water buffalo.'

"While the rest of China has been plagued, year after year, by starvation, Shu-Hsa-Pa has not had famine in almost a century. The Shui-hsa—the dawn redwood—may well be a very lucky tree!

"Appearance of the dawn redwood area is how Alaska, Greenland and Spitzbergen looked 100,000,000 years ago, when those Arctic lands were warm and lush and green, and when the United States was covered by a tropical sea.

"Fossil remains of these ancient trees have been found preserved together in rocks 100,000,000 years old in the Arctic, in rocks 60,000,000 years old in Japan, in rocks 40,000,000 years old in Switzerland, and in rocks 30,000,000 years old in the Northwestern United States.

"Fossilized leaves and cones have been found all over the northern hemisphere—in Greenland, Iceland, the British Isles, Germany, Switzerland, Scandinavia, Siberia, Northern China, Japan, the Aleutians, Alaska, Canada and the United States from Eastern Oregon to New Jersey.

"Strange things have happened to the world map since the Cretaceous period. Then the Mediterranean area was engulfed by an enormous sea, the Tethys, which covered what is now North Africa, France, Germany, South Russia, the Balkans, most of Italy and even Switzerland. Tibet, Afghanistan, Persia, and Malay peninsula and Southern China were under water and a sea divided India into two parts—one of which connected with Africa.

"In America, the so-called Cordilleran sea covered what is now the Rocky Mountain states. Most of California, Oregon and Washington was under the Pacific. The enormous Aleutian land bridge joined Alaska and Siberia. There were no Alps, no Himalayas, no Andes.

"During Cretaceous times, the northern parts of Europe, Asia and America had balmy, temperate climates—much like that of Oregon and Northern California today—or dawn redwoods would not have lived there. As thousands of centuries passed, however, Arctic winters began to get colder. Many species of plants died out or "migrated" southward. The dawn redwood probably lasted longer than other cone-bearing trees, since it has the remarkable habit of dropping its leaves in winter—a life-saving device in severe cold.

"At the same time the Tethys and Cordilleran seas and other ancient bodies of water shrank or disappeared entirely, uncovering millions of square miles of new land. Many plant species which died out in the freezing Arctic were able to invade these new territories. As California and Oregon emerged from the Pacific, they provided fertile soil for the dawn redwoods and for their surprising offspring, the modern redwoods.

"'But after about 80,000,000 years of this remarkable migration, it seemed as if the dawn redwoods had been wiped out,' Dr. Chaney explained. 'They were totally gone from Europe. They were gone from Siberia, Japan and North China. They had disappeared from Alaska and the rest of North America, leaving only the California and Oregon redwoods as their surviving descendants.'

"Yet, fantastically, the dawn redwoods had not entirely vanished. They made one last stand in Central China.

SEEDLINGS:

Brought to America,
Planted by Professor

"And there in China, the powerful forces of nature came to their aid. The earth around them was pulled and heaved and forced upward, and enormous ranges of mountains were created. These mountains provided sanctuary. They changed the direction of the winds, they kept these few valleys warm and drenched with rain every month in the year, and—millions of years later—they acted as barriers to men who came with axes and saws.

"'I can think of no other plant or animal,' Dr. Chaney said, 'which has fought so long to survive and which is so perilously close to extinction.'

"In the Valley of the Tiger, there are more than 100 big dawn redwoods, many of them 80 or 90 or even 100 feet tall. Around them grow wild modern plants—azaleas, rhododendrons, hydrangeas, iris, wild strawberries, Chinese yew, clumps of bamboo and tall Cunninghamia trees.

"Dr. Chaney arrived in Nanking safely after eluding Chinese bandits along the Szschuan-Hupeh border. One bandit was shot and killed by the expedition's escort of Chinese soldiers near the village of Lung-chu-pa. Two others are believed to have been wounded, but both escaped.

"At Nanking, Dr. Chaney sought government and scientific support for preserving the small forest of dawn redwoods near Shuissa-pa. Virtually the last stand of the ancient trees anywhere in the world, this forest now is being cut for timber by local farmers.

"'I know China is desperate for wood,' said Dr. Chaney, 'but it seems unthinkable that the last of these ancient trees should be destroyed.'

"Dr. Chaney talked to the head man of Shui-hsa-pa, an elder called Wu Tsaming, and urged him to protect the dawn redwoods growing in the valley of the Tiger near by. Wu explained his people's need for wood and said the problem must be settled by 'higher authorities.'

Accordingly, Dr. Chaney went to the Chinese capital to place his appeal before that nation's leaders. Some samples were analyzed at Nanking, but Dr. Chaney brought some to the United States for investigation by American experts. Wood of the dawn redwoods appears to be lighter in weight and softer than modern redwood. The outer portions are whitish, while the inner resembles the color of bleached bricks.

"In the villages near dawn redwood stands, the wood is used primarily for interior finishes. It is not yet known if it has the amazing resistance to termites and other insects which characterizes the redwoods of California and Oregon, but eventually Dr. Chaney thinks this will be determined.

"Now dawn redwoods are growing in America again—after an absence of about 25,000,000 years. Four of them, young seedlings ranging from 6 to 15 inches in height have been planted in Berkeley, Cal., by Chaney. They will be guarded in greenhouses, tended and nurtured and deluged with vitamins. They are probably the most precious of botanical specimens in America today."

GINKGO
petrified forest

The Ginkgo Petrified Forest, located on U.S. Highway 10 . . . approximately two miles west of Vantage, (Washington) represents one of the most unusual fossil localities in the world. Entombed in the basaltic lava flows of the hills lie the remains of a forest which flourished and died millions of years ago. Few fossil beds yield a flora so diversed as that represented by the species found at Ginkgo, and only rarely are fossils preserved in the lava flows.

In the basalt lie thousands of petrified logs, the cell structure so perfectly preserved that it has been possible to identify more than fifty genera and two hundred species. These fossil woods include some types extinct long before the arrival of man and many others still living today. Among them are logs of the ginkgo for which the area is named.

The ginkgo, last surviving member of a family which first appeared some 200 million years ago, is now a popular ornamental tree. This "living fossil" apparently escaped extinction only because the Chinese Buddhists cultivated it for centuries in their temple grounds. Though Ginkgo leaves have been collected from many parts of the world, only in a few areas has petrified Ginkgo wood been found.

Geologic events leading to preservation of these logs go back 15 or 20 million years, before uplift of the Cascade mountains, to what geologists call the Miocene epoch. During the Miocene, great floods of basaltic lava welled quietly up through deep cracks of fissures in the earth's crust, spreading rapidly over the landscape. In the long intervals between some of the eruptions, streams blocked by the lava flows backed up to form lakes and marshes. Through the years soil accumulated. Trees, such as cypress in the swamps and hardwoods in the upland regions, grew rapidly, nourished by moisture laden winds from the Pacific Ocean.

From northern highlands, logs of spruce, fir, pine and sequoia were swept down the rivers at flood stage. Here they lodged on lake shores and in cypress swamps, the logs mingled with those of hardwoods, such as oak and elm. In time, volcanic fissures opened again, and the lava flowed over the swamps, lakes and streams with their accumulation of logs of many species. Eventually, repeated lava eruptions built up to a thickness exceeding two miles, producing one of the great lava fields of the world—the Columbia Plateau.

Article appeared in Washington State Travel Book of 1962.

Water seeping down through the lavas carried silica which penetrated the buried logs. The wood fibers were impregnated and encased by silica causing their present rock-like condition. Mineral impurities in the silica gave the petrified logs their bright coloring—red, brown, yellow or white.

At the close of the Miocene epoch, uplift of the Cascade mountains cut off the moist winds from the west, leaving eastern Washington in its present desert state. In the millions of years since the Miocene, the lavas have been folded and broken by pressures within the earth's crust. Erosion by rivers and floods from melting glaciers cut into the lava plateau, down through one flow after another, exposing the logs as we see them today. Buried by basaltic lava, encased in silica, and exposed by eroding streams and glacial waters, the logs of Ginkgo Petrified Forest remain in testimony to the moist climate and lush forests of central Washington millions of years ago.

Preservation of the scientific remains was inaugurated in 1934, when the first tract of state land was set aside to protect the unusually rich exposures of petrified logs and the exceptional variety of fossil woods in this locality. Although fossil woods had been reported from the Columbia Plateau as far back as 1898, this area was not well known until 1931, when it was brought to public attention by Professor George F. Beck of the Central Washington College at Ellensburg.

Development was initiated through a cooperative program involving the State of Washington, the National Park Service and the Civilian Conservation Corps. Since that time the State Park and Recreation Commission has built the present museum and developed exhibits which interpret the geologic story. Many polished specimens of petrified wood from the area are displayed, including the outstanding F.W. Bobo collection. Partially excavated petrified logs may be seen in their natural setting at the park trailsite, located 2½ miles west of the museum on U.S. Highway 10. This state park covers an area of approximately 6,000 acres. No collecting of petrified wood is allowed in the park, but similar material may be found in the eastern part of Kittitas county.

Petrified wood may be found near Sunnyside, Washington, a few miles south of the Yakima-Cold Springs road (see map). Other areas are at Trinidad near Grant county; in the Rattlesnake Hills and Horse Heaven Hills in lower Benton county; on the Ellensburg-Yakima highway (U.S. Highway 97) in the area approximately four to 12 miles north of Yakima. This area is in steep canyon country and care should be used in climbing. During the summer months there is a heavy infestation of rattlesnakes. Small deposits of petrified wood are also found in the Chehalis area; between Othello and Beverly on the north side of the Saddle Mountains (Grant County) and along the Chinook Pass Highway (U.S. Highway 410).

Indian petroglyphs included in the Ginkgo Forest Museum were obtained from basalt cliffs along the Columbia River in the vicinity of Vantage. Such petroglyphs, sometimes called "picture rocks", are cut or pecked into stone, and represent art work of early Indian inhabitants of the Columbia Plateau. The

Ginkgo biloba (opposite), long thought to exist only as fossil curiosity, was discovered as revered temple tree in China and Japan where it reaches 150′ in height. Introduced into New World, graceful ginkgo has prospered under variety of common names such as maidenhair tree, Kew tree (probably first introduced in Kew Gardens, London, England). Specimen shown here, largest in Portland, Oregon, partly because of three-pronged trunk, flourishes near Lloyd Center. Although tree normally turns soft yellow in fall this one photographed in late November, is barely coloring at extreme top.

precise meaning or intention of these drawings is a riddle not yet solved. A rich area archeologically, evidence of human habitation extending back at least 10,000 years ago has been found. Implements left by these people include many artifacts made from petrified wood, and arrowheads unexcelled in their beauty, symmetry and fine workmanship. With the completion of the Wanapum Dam, 6 miles downstream from Vantage, these specimens would have been covered by water had they not been salvaged.

The museum is closed during the months of December and January. During the summer months the hours are 8 a.m. to 7 p.m. daily and 9 a.m. to 5 p.m. during the winter months, weather permitting.

The only known petrified ginkgo trees in the world, says Mrs. Rex. R. Campbell, are found in the Ginkgo Petrified Forest State Park at Vantage, north and east of Yakima. The park includes an estimated 10,000 petrified trees, including oak, maple, walnut, redwood, swamp cypress, Douglas fir and a number of others as well as the ginkgo, of which only six specimens have been reported.

One of the oldest and most primitive types of trees, the ginkgo has been preserved and handed down from the Orient.

Most of the petrified wood in central Washington is opalized, but some is found to be agate. Petrified woods usually take a high polish and are eminently suited for the making of jewelry and ornaments of various kinds.

Book ends cut from petrified wood are attractive and useful, the art of the lapidarist bringing out the grain and other marks.

With a microscope (50 power is ample for ordinary work) and a little study one can determine the species or type of wood. Hard woods such as oak, walnut and hickory have prominent medullary (marrow) rays radiating out from the center of the cross section and cutting across the annular rings.

Collectors prefer to identify the specimens by species rather than merely labeling them petrified wood.

How were the petrified woods formed? When the magmatic waters from deep in the earth mixed with juvenile or middle waters and were met by surface water, a slight drop in temperature resulted in the surface waters depositing combinations of silica, alkali, acid and mineral salt. The complicated action resulting was no doubt the petrifying agent.

The wood (cellulose) was probably literally digested and replaced with a silica jell and the liquid mineral solutions. Attempts to petrify wood artificially have failed; nature alone holds the secret.

Fruits of ginkgo are pale amber in color, these shown about 1″ long. Pulp exudes odor variously described as from "bad" to "putrid", author deeming it simply unpleasant. Encased is good sized, almond shaped cream and orange colored nut containing very pleasant tasting kernel, these said to be important food item in native China.

Middle reaches of Columbia River present very different aspect from mountainous upper and densely forested lower areas. Here at Ginkgo Petrified Forest Museum, near Vantage, Washington, on high rim rock shelf, is display of petrified logs of many species. The 200 or more species represented could never have grown in this one area, although many climates have come and gone over eons of time. Explanation for abundance of species is that in ancient times many violent floods carried tons of varied types of trees which lodged here and were later covered by lava flows and eventually petrified. It is said that area is only one in which petrified logs are found encased in lava. Background here clearly shows evidence of many lava flows, each separated by very long periods of time. Particular layer here can be followed up, down and across Columbia and is termed for convenience the "Museum flow."

Close up of ginkgo foliage reveals in divided leaves basis for scientific name, *Ginkgo biloba*.

One individual "tree" *(above left)* clearly shows grain of ancient wood, especially at top where annual rings show.

Collection of more than 150 tons of petrified wood *(above)* is almost unbelievable. Columbia is barren, rock-walled river here and logs are seen by few visitors. Rough, rocky, narrow road leads 12 miles from Vantage, Washington, surface "home made" with 6% grade for half mile. Driving author to log collection, Clarence Scammon required 2 hours each way in ancient Ford pickup.

Cross-cut slice of log thought to be spruce shows annual rings more distinctly than in actual wood. Spectacular piece is among many owned by the Scammons.

Last of new colored leaves here cling to almost naked branches of ginkgo like so many yellow butterflies. Two days later all were fallen, ground beneath covered with rich golden carpet.

Clarence and Florence Scammon greeting author at Scammon's Landing, Washington, (little dock in background). Couple has lived here well over 40 years, Clarence having spent much of his time excavating with pick and shovel, hauling heavy logs down steep cliffs, reerecting them with block and tackle. Residence is small, most space occupied with a wealth of historic museum artifacts.

"That Crooked Sapling" they first called the oak, *Quercus Garryana*. It later bore several more dignified titles—Lover's Oak, The Camelback Tree, Arch Tree and finally The Praying Oak. It was once featured in Ripley's "Believe It or Not" column. This photo and drawing with much of the story were included in a small brochure prepared in celebration of Oregon Centennial by Oregon Roadside Council and not more specially credited. (Data and photos courtesy Milwaukie Historical Society.)

The
PRAYING OAK

A fast running river enters the Columbia River at a point near the small town of Troutdale, Oregon. The stream is turgid with glacial grit and was inevitably termed Sandy River. Source of its icy water is a large glacier on the west side of Mount Hood and named for the river it generates. During most of the stream's route from mountain to Columbia its flow is constricted to narrow, heavily wooded canyons, widening only slightly to a small "flood plain" just before emptying itself into the Columbia.

Sometime in the early 1850s a pioneer family settled on the west bank, finding there a beautiful grove of oaks with fertile lands intermingled. Some of the ground was left clear for pasture and soon began "reforesting" itself, the random mixture of native growth including a seedling oak.

About the year 1860 the land was sold to neighbor who owned the adjoining homestead and in 1863 the whole was taken over by Captain James Menzies and later called the Sundial Ranch. In 1879 Captain Menzies decided to put the land under cultivation. Later he wrote of his first sight of the "Praying Oak."

"My brother Wilbur and I set posts and built the new north line fence along the south side of the road. One day we ate our lunch and sat by the side of the road, sitting on a log. After lunch I went to investigate the layer of drift of which the log was a part.

"Not far away I found the 'oak sapling' bent over a rotten log left by the homesteader, then to the ground under a drift log; the top of the sapling was growing up between this log and the one laying by it. I called to my brother to come and see the oak sapling. It was about four inches in diameter. Its serpentine curves made such an impression on me that it was never forgotten."

"For several years after that I traveled to the upper ford of the little Sandy River where the cows rested after a day in the pasture, to start them home. Often I rode off the road to see the bent sapling and watch its growth. If the new road had been built on the old line the sapling would have been cut down.

We used to gather our winter's supply of hazel nuts from that piece of land. The homesteader's house and barn were on the northeast corner of the field about fifty feet from the bank of the river. When I think of the barn I see hanging on a wooden peg a worn out set of harnesses with chain tugs, belly and back bands encased in leather, relics of their long treck on the Oregon Trail and their part in the carving out of the field."

In 1889 the Sandy Ranch was sold to D.L. Gee who cut off all the timber that was marketable. The slash was burned and the ground leveled. Long before this ruthless clearing of the land the curiously bent young oak was known and loved by all the settlers in the area. All expected the tree to be destroyed in the process. But when the smoke from the burning cleared the Praying Tree was seen to kneel as before, unscathed by axe or fire.

By 1941 the tree was famous for miles around, the citizens of Troutdale especially revering the oak, by now a sturdy specimen. Then came an even more serious threat. The United States Government was cooperating in the establishment of the huge Reynolds aluminum plant. Would the threatened removal of all wild growth from the property now destroy the Praying Oak? Enraged Troutdale citizens banded together to petition the government and Reynolds Aluminum Reduction Plant to spare and protect the landmark. Final result was a company statement that it would be preserved and surrounded with a stout fence.

Stout or not, the enclosure was of no avail against the final disaster. On October 12, 1962 a windstorm of unprecedented force struck the entire Northwest coastal area, doing untold damage. Among casualties was the Praying Oak, torn from the ground and tossed some distance away. Present efforts to locate any remaining debris have been without success.

How Praying Oak was formed—Columbia River has always been subject to major flooding in May and June when snow melts in its enormous mountain watershed. In June 1876 it reached a higher stage than in any freshets in memory of oldest settlers. As flood waters backed up into Sandy River flood plain they were met by smaller but surging flood rushing down that stream. Waters rose over Capt. Menzies' ranch at rate of 2 feet per hour until they covered ranch house floor several inches. Huge drifts of floating logs settled on farm lands, one catching little sapling, bearing it to ground. Eventually all drift logs rotted away or were removed.

Landmark
APPLE TREE

After almost 150 years of strenuous, adventuresome life "The Old Apple Tree", a national historic site, grown from seeds brought from England by a British officer, is still bearing fruit and attracting more attention than all those commercially grown apples in a state famous for them. Let Carl Landerholm tell the story in his own way.

"Apples, and in general our common fruit trees, were not indigenous to the old Oregon Country, of which our state is a part. Horticulture here is definitely a contribution of the white man, and the first fruit trees planted were in the present state of Washington, at the old Hudson's Bay Company's Fort Vancouver. The most probable date of this first planting is 1827, certainly not later. The present year, 1952, would therefore mark a century and a quarter of apple growing in this part of the world.

Unfortunately for the propagation of exact history, events later proving to be of great interest often are not recognized as extraordinary when they happen. No diarist recorded that first planting. We must therefore rely upon incidental remarks of occasional travelers of the period, or upon memories perhaps a bit dimmed by intervening years. This much is clear—that our first apples were grown from seeds and that a number of sources point to Lieutenant A. Emilius Simpson, in the employ of the Hudson's Bay Company, as the bearer of the seeds from England. One such source tells the story as follows: 'The first fruit tree grown on the Columbia sprang from the seed of an apple eaten at a dinner-party in London. The dinner had been given to Captain Lieutenant Simpson, of the Company's coast service. One of the ladies present, more in jest than in earnest, took from the apples brought on with the dessert, the seeds; and dropping them into Simpson's pocket, told him to plant them when he should reach his Northwest wilderness. The captain had forgotten the circumstance until reminded of it while dining at Fort Vancouver in 1827, by finding in the pocket of the waistcost which he had worn last in London, the seeds playfully put in by his lady friend. Taking them out he gave them to Bruce the gardener, who carefully planted them; and thence within the territory of Oregon began the growth of apple trees." Another chronicler, writing in later years, is however more specific about the disposal of the seeds: 'My father and Mr. Pambrun and Simpson were together, and they three planted them in little boxes. They kept little boxes in the store somewhere where they could not be touched, and put glass over them. I do not know how long they were there. They were all green, and by and by we got apples. At first there was only one apple on the tree. It was a great treat, for everybody had just a little slice. There was a good many it had to go around among.' Clearly, between the episode of the little boxes and that of the little slices some years must have intervened.

Jedediah Smith, American trapper and adventurer, coming up from the Umpqua River, arrived at Fort Vancouver on August 8, 1828, 'unheralded and without credentials'. Generous Chief Factor John McLoughlin took him in and lodged him for some months without charge. He certifies that there were 'some small apples and grape vines' growing there then. The Reverend Jonathan S. Green in his missionary report on Oregon, 1829, tells of meeting Leiutenant Simpson in Hawaii who said that he had planted grapes and apples in Oregon, and 'they appeared to be flourishing.'

Mrs. Narcissa Prentiss Whitman, wife of Dr. Marcus Whitman and one of the two first American women to cross the plains to Oregon, arrived at Fort Vancouver on September 12, 1836. Her diary contains the following entry: 'What a delightful place this is; what a contrast to the rough, barren sand plains through which we have so recently passed. Here we find fruit of every description—apples, peaches, grapes, pears, plums, and fig trees in abundance;—Here I must mention the origin of these grapes and apples. A gentleman, twelve years ago, while at a party in London, put the seeds of grapes and apples into his vest pocket; soon afterwards he took a voyage to this country and left them here, and now they are greatly multiplied.' The 'twelve years ago' is clearly an error, as the original fort at Vancouver was not built until the following winter 1824-1825. Furthermore, Lieutenant Simpson did not arrive at Fort Vancouver until November 2, 1826. Under date of October 25, 1836 Mrs. Whitman wrote: 'The grapes are just ripe and I am feasting on them finely.—I save all the seeds of those I eat for planting and *of apples* also. This is the rule of Vancouver.'

Apple culture in the Pacific Northwest, in short, began about one hundred twenty five years ago. The place was Fort Vancouver. The method of propagation was by seeds; and this method continued for some time,

Is there any survivor of this long ago first planting?

Near the southwest corner of the old military reservation at Vancouver, Washington, a couple of hundred yards from the Columbia River and just north of the Evergreen Highway stands an aged apple tree, obviously a seedling. It is inclosed by a concrete and chain fence, near which is a marker bearing the following legend:

THE OLDEST APPLE TREE
IN THE PACIFIC NORTHWEST.
THE SEED WAS BROUGHT FROM
ENGLAND AND PLANTED BY THE
HUDSON BAY COMPANY
IN THE YEAR 1826.

Known and loved as "The Old Apple Tree" *(opposite),* this specimen has suffered much as have other vegetative ancients. Most damage was done in notorious Columbus Day storm when tree was literally cut in half. After small planting area was added to Vancouver (Washington) City Park System, Mayor Rudy Luepke, son of pioneer florist in the city, saw to it that damage was corrected, this necessitating removal of major damaged portion, reducing size of tree. Other forms of surgery have been performed over the years. Luepke officiated at dedication in 1962 of monument and descriptive plaque placed by Vancouver Historical Society.

The credit for having the fence built and other protective measures taken to preserve the tree goes to the late E.L. French, Clark County orchardist and at one time state Director of agriculture. Early in 1911 Mr. French, then state senator, first interested himself in the matter. He called upon A.A. Quarnberg, then county Horticulturist, and asked the latter to take steps to save the long neglected and all-but-forgotten tree. Mr. Quarnberg in turn convinced Colonel George K. McGunnegle, commander of the Barracks, that the tree was indeed of the first planting, with the result that orders were issued to preserve it.

Again memory and circumstance must be brought into play to substantiate as far as they may that the old apple tree is truly a genuine 'first'. At the outset one notes the startling fact that the tree stands approximately a half mile southwest of where the historic orchard, mentioned by Mrs. Whitman and numerous others, stood. Their statements and the comtemporary maps show that this orchard was located just north of the stockage, and the tree is quite isolated from any other former orchard! Because of this, doubts have been expressed regarding the claim. For instance, about 1925 the late George H. Himes of the Oregon Historical Society thought that the tree was a descendant rather than an ancestor of the Hudson's Bay Company orchard. But, paradoxically, the location and isolation of the tree really argues for, rather than against, its priority; for, when the seeds were planted—in 1826 or 1827—the original fort on the hill at the site of the present State School for the Deaf was still the only establishment at Vancouver. There is no evidence of any fruit trees being planted there. The historic stockade, located over a mile west, on the plain, was not constructed until the spring of 1829. Hence the planting of the orchard there would hardly have occurred before the following summer of 1829, or two years and over after the seeds brought by Simpson were planted. Furthermore, the Old Apple Tree stands on ground high enough to be pretty well out of reach of river floods, to the west and very close to where the road passed from the Hudson's Bay Company wharf to the original and later fort alike, and only a short distance from the wharf. It seems to be almost an ideal spot for that first planting: A well watered place, but level and elevated enough to be free from overflow and adjacent to the only road to the fort.

A Vancouver newspaper dated May 17, 1883 carries the following item: The first apple trees in Oregon are described in the Oregon City *Enterprise* in the following interesting reminiscence: 'The first apple tree on the Pacific coast was raised from the seed. The seed was obtained from six apples which had been sent out on a Hudson Bay Company's ship from England to Vancouver. Mr. P.C. Pambrun, father to Mrs. Dr. Barclay of our city (Oregon City), was the gentleman who had the honor of being the first to plant a tame apple tree that bore fruit. This was done in the year 1826—.We wonder if any of the trees are yet standing at Vancouver?'

Old Emporer Alexander *(opposite)* grows, blooms and still bears heavily each September on author's grounds. Tree is almost certainly from grafted specimen first brought to Oregon by Henderson Llewelling in 1847, site of his old nursery not far away. Apples of this variety are large, beautifully striped with red, not of best keeping quality. Almost all old varieties had serious drawbacks, most remedied by modern methods, some by exhaustive efforts in hybridization, some like Red Delicious by purest chance.

In answer to the above inquiry we are informed by a gentleman who has lived in Vancouver for 30 years, or since about 1853, that two of the original apple trees are still standing on the government reserve."

The writer of this present article inquired of one of the present directors of the Fort Vancouver Restoration and Historical Society, who spent much of her girlhood, during the 1880's, at the military reservation, whether she knew anything about the tree then. She replied affirmatively. She recalls *two* trees, one of which is the Old Apple Tree. They were regularly referred to as 'The old apple trees' even then; and she states that for some seasons she and other gathered fruit for household use from them.

Another writer of more recent times (1938) states that there were originally five trees from the first planting, but does not give the source of information; and states further that the one tree was spared in 1894 from the fate of the rest because of a kind-hearted sergeant found a robin's nest in its branches. She qualifies the last assertion by saying that it is 'as legend goes'.

The above clues to the authenticity of the claims for the venerable old apple tree hang together pretty well and are all favorable, save the opinion of Mr. Himes, which I have discussed, and indicated that his very objection is really a strong point *in favor of* the claims. Finally, no other explanation for this ancient tree at that place has ever, as far as I know, been advanced. We can, I believe, safely say that the apple culture of the Pacific Northwest began at that little inclosure.

(Signed) Carl Landerholm

The Vancouver *Columbian* gives a later account of the famous tree in its issue of November 26, 1972, the article "Old Apple Tree Survives Storms and Still Bears Fruit", written by Harley Mays.

"In January, 1950, the Columbian carried the distressing news that the old historic apple tree (at the Camas Highway—Interstate 5 intersection) had suffered a serious injury and was probably beyond recovery. As a result of a heavy layer of ice caused by subzero temperatures, one of its two main limbs was broken and lying on the ground.

This was no ordinary tree. It was grown from seed brought from England and planted by employees of the Hudson's Bay Company in 1827, according to reliable accounts.

Since this outpost was then the only substantial settlement in the region occupied by white man the apple tree is the only living thing known to have been planted by man in this vast territory, an area reaching from central California to the frozen north and from the Rocky Mountains to the Pacific Ocean.

Because of an intense interest in trees of all kinds, and having some experience in caring for them, I decided to look at the broken tree and see if anything could be done to save it. Standing forlornly beside an army coal supply yard, the historic tree was located on military barracks property and it was soon determined that there were no plans to remedy its condition.

Since the tree was growing on government property, it was necessary to get permission to work on it. A hurriedly arranged meeting between Mayor Vern Anderson, Donald Stewart, president of the historical society, and the commanding officer of the barracks produced the authorization.

It soon became apparent that the trunk of the old tree was a hollow shell that had been filled with concrete by some unknown benefactor many years before. The concrete core which was intended to strengthen the trunk had been broken to bits by the buffeting of storms and was intermingled with decaying wood which harbored an assortment of insects. To save the tree, it would be necessary to remove all the broken concrete and rotten wood to prevent the spread of decay into the solid portion of the trunk. Special tools had to be made which could be thrust through holes made by limbs broken long ago. The tedious process began.

In the early stages of the operation, Dave Almendinger, director of the Southwest Washington Experimental Station, offered his services within the limits of his time. Paul Wesseler, County Extension Agent, was a frequent visitor to the site.

It required many days to remove the large quantity of waste material. The trunk stood like a hollow chimney with the interior accessible through the large hole at the top caused by the broken limb.

After disinfecting and coating the sound wood which remained, it became necessary to stabilize the fragile trunk which would otherwise fall easy prey to the first heavy windstorm. To again fill the trunk with concrete would only encourage the spread of decay and greatly shorten the life of the tree.

We decided to use a heavy steel pipe, which was inserted into the center of the hollow trunk and anchored by a footing of concrete below the ground level. It was an unusual type of "open heart" surgery.

The outward appearance of the tree was restored to its original condition, and the strength of the invisible support was demonstrated by the Columbus Day

Springtime apple blossoms belie ancient lineage of variety, Emperor Alexander, originally imported from Russia with once well known Red Astrachan and first reported in U.S. in 1832.

Cherry blossoms in December? These were cut from rather rare specimen of *Prunus subhirtella autumnalis* on author's grounds in winter. Some blossoms regularly appear before all leaves are shed, then showing on bare twigs wealth of dainty light pink until hard frosts temporarily stop flowering. Successive spells of milder weather throughout winter produce some flowers, then finally a last burst in spring.

windstorm, which toppled many young and vigorous trees in the vicinity. Annual inspections have been made and periodic treatments have prevented decay or the invasion of damaging insects.

Twenty-two years have passed since that disastrous winter and the growth of the tree has been phenomenal. The apple tree has greatly increased in size and bears a crop of apples comparable to trees in their prime, indicating that the old Hudson's Bay apple tree will be with us for many years to come.

Such woody plants as fruits, roses and many others reproduce themselves in two ways, by seeds and by asexual means—by the extension of the tree or plant by its own wood through grafting or cutting. It is often said that 'like begets like' but in the case of plant seeds from parents of mixed lineage, meaning hybrids, results are very chancy. In most cases progency revert to the characteristics of an ancestor or mixture of several. Roses so produced are likely to be small, single or lacking attributes desired by most fanciers, apples and other fruits lacking the virtues of their immediate parents.

In rare instances, perhaps one in many hundreds or even thousands, a seedling rose will produce a blossom like none every seen before, or a seedling apple may yield fruit to revolutionize the orchard industry. Such an apple was the Red Delicious, a chance seedling probably resulting from a cross between two old timers, bellflower and winesap. This young tree appearing in the back yard of Jesse Hiatt of Winterset, Iowa, and first seen in public in 1892, was to produce through grafting well over 10 million trees at last count, and these through one nursery only—Stark's. Estimates are that $100 million worth of this fruit is sold annually.

Vancouver's old apple tree is a seedling and although not destined to produce a whole new race of apples, has been famous for a long time through sheer longevity, surviving many near brushes with death by vagaries of weather and man's frequent assaults in the building of roads, airports.

Plantings in the west were made much earlier in the southern sector. Date palms, olives and fruiting cacti were planted with the building of the missions in California. Apples do not thrive there except in mountain areas cold enough to allow a period of dormancy. (Apples grown at Julian in the Cuyamacas were exotic delicacies in San Diego in later years).

Certainly the Vancouver apple was not the first to be planted west of the Mississippi. An historic incident is described in 'The Stark Story', special publication of the Missouri Historical Society *Bulletin* of September 1966.

'It was near sundown on the evening of October 10, in the year 1816, when a small band of settlers, weary after days of travel in wagons and on horseback from their native Kentucky, crossed the Mississippi River at a point where the town of Louisiana, in Pike County, Missouri, is now situated, and made camp.

Autumn was in the air, and as they looked back at the bluffs and slopes leading down to the river they had just crossed, and then towards the west with the rolling hills and forests touched by autumn colors, they liked what they saw.

One of the leaders of the group was a twenty-four year old man of medium build and stern expression named James Hart Stark. He had visited this area a year earlier as a member of a scouting and surveying party and had decided that here was where he wanted to live and rear his family.

As the travelers prepared to make camp that night, James Stark untied from his saddle what appeared to be a bundle of switches. They were important to him, but he little dreamed how important they were to become, not just to him, but to future generations of the Stark family, and to the whole world of horticulture. The switches were in fact a bundle of apple scions from his father's farm in Bourbon County, Kentucky, scions which when grafted to wild crab apple trees, would grow some of the first cultivated fruit west of the Mississippi, and

42

which would spread over the midwest, the Missouri and the Mississippi valleys, later into the Far West, and finally over all the world.

Not too many years after this incident seeds of Vancouver's Old Apple Tree were planted and the tree was flourishing when William Barlow jettisoned his apple tree stock at The Dalles, Oregon. James J. Weeks, former president of Waso County (Oregon), tells the story in the Centennial Edition of *The Barlow Road*. The Vancouver tree was producing fruit of fair quality and could have been responsible for the statements of men who had been across the Cascades in Oregon and for the subsequent dumping of the Barlow trees.

'One of the interesting sidelights of the younger Barlow's *Reminiscences*' involves an altogether unrelated but tremendously significant aspect of Oregon history, particularly in development of the State's horticulture.

Keenly interested in fruit growing, William had brought a peck of apple seeds from the plains and planted them after buying squatter's rights to a section of land on the Clackamas River.

But his near claim to horticultural fame involved grafted fruit tree stock contained in a 300-pound box of dirt which he also had when the journey started. Barlow described the trees as representative of the finest Illinois had to offer.

The trees did not make it to Oregon, however, While Barlow was in the Rockies on the trip west he was told by men who had been across the Cascades that Oregon already had the finest fruit in the world, that he ought to get rid of the box to eliminate needless weight, and that in any event he would have to put his possessions on a raft to go downriver once he got to The Dalles. The combination seemed to present problems, so Barlow dumped the box on the ground.

As things turned out, Barlow discovered when he reached the Willamette Valley there were no grafted fruit trees in that area, or in California. If he had taken his young trees with him and safely crossed the mountains with them he could have made a full monopoly of all the grafted apples and pears on the coast . . . ' "

During years of eucalyptus boom in California vast groves of Australian import were set out in haze of rosy dreams of great fortunes soon to come. The years brought bitter disillusionment, trees cut down by the thousands or left to die of overcrowding, lack of water. Some were cut and recut for firewood as stumps regenerated growth. This truncated grove surrounds rest stop on U.S. Highway 5 in Sacramento Valley.

BOOM AND BUST
in California

Some time after the turn of the century foresters, lumbermen and get-rich-quick promoters went wild over the idea of planting immense groves of Australian eucalyptus trees in California. Rewards would be quickly realized, they said. The rapidly growing hardwood trees could be cut down in a very few years, yielding valuable "gumwood" for fine furniture.

The trees did grow rapidly, producing as much as 4,000 cubic feet in timber or wood per acre in a ten-year rotation. But disillusionment came when attempts were made to cure the green timber properly. The relatively soft wood (in some species), when first felled, hardened quickly to defy axe and saw. In the fastest growing species (more than 300 classified ones in all) there were rotten or hollow cores. The outer, sapwood, dried or cured at a different rate than the heartwood. Some of these difficulties were gradually eliminated at great cost but the market soon became flooded with far more gumwood than local furniture makers could hope to use.

As prices fell to a record low and the Great Depression hit, most flourishing eucalyptus groves were cut down for firewood for which the logs were perfectly suited. (Today some are processed into charcoal briquettes for outdoor cooking). Since the remaining stumps quickly coppiced into new, closely growing trees, many were not removed but left to continue production of firewood and fence posts. Others were neglected, left to grow into disreputable groves that finally died for lack of moisture. Other old groves and many single trees have suffered greatly in recent years of declining rainfall and drought. In some extreme northern sections of California, as near Crescent City, the trees were recently injured fatally during cold winters. Yet the ubiquitous eucalyptus is a most conspicuous and utilitarian tree, virtually a symbol of California.

In 1975 the author saw many stumps apparently dead that were sending out year-old shoots from bases six feet high. With sufficient water, either by rainfall or artifically provided, the California eucalyptus trees are the most striking, varied and easily cared for trees in the state.

Eucalyptus trees were first noted in Australia by British botanists and the reports of the gigantic trees native there, in Tasmania and neighboring restricted areas reached London sometime in the early 1880s. Nobody knows when the first one was planted in California but the *California Historical Society Quarterly* of June, 1937, reports one giant planted in 1867. This specimen stood near Napa and then measured 10 feet in diameter and 30 feet in circumference 5 feet from the ground. It was said to have grown to 30 feet tall by 1870.

The eucalyptus (called simply "eucalypt" in Australia) is as different from the native California redwood as any tree could be but the tallest trees in the world and the tallest hardwood (easily 300 feet where it is native) have at least one feature in common. In spite of the tremendous dimensions achieved by both, they share the distinction of having extremely small seeds, many thousands to the pound. The author found seeds of the popular *E. cinera*, "Spiral", germinating in his greenhouse in five days—nearly 100% of them. The seeds obviously retain good viability, having survived the long voyages in sailing vessels when first exported from the island continent.

Various species of eucalyptus *(extreme left)* take many forms in height, bark furrowed or smooth, leaves narrow, lanceolate, round or broad. One form is shown at close range, trunk nestling in multitude of African daisies. Border of these giant trees ring huge parking lot for old but still elegant Hotel Del Coronado, Coronado, California.

Row of smooth-trunked eucalyptus *(below)* borders golf course in Coronado. Soft focus enhances airy effect of open growth in this species.

Eucalyptus viminalis. This old photo *(below)* from Bailey's *Horticultural Encyclopedia* is used here to show how large some species can become. The type was once much grown as very floriferous bee tree but escaped boom for furniture as wood is weak and brittle.

Famed missions of California, in addition to main objective, proselyting the native Indians, was to stop southward thrust of Russian settlements in California. On May 5, 1812, Ivan Alexander Kuskof began building of fort on coast of Northern California, naming it Rossiya for Russia, settlement becoming known as Fort Ross. Ironically, when the most northern missions, San Rafael and San Francisco Solano were established, Russians instead of displaying any enmity toward the padres, visited them and soon established a lively trade with them. However, with the decimation of sea otters and consequent end to their main income from fur trade, Russians turned to ship building, constructing four vessels of green oak timber. The wood decayed so rapidly as to doom that venture also, and in 1824 colonists agreed to limit further expansion to Alaska. Abandoned were many substantial farm and other buildings. One of ranches at Fort Ross became property of Call family.

Carlos A. Call, shown in photo, said his father had planted this eucalyptus tree about 1875. Others in the photo are, at left Juanita McGraw and right Jeanette Rosson. The tree is reputed to be largest eucalyptus in Sonoma County, possibly in state. Its buttress measured 52 feet in contoured circumference at 2½ feet above the ground. (Photo by Larry L. McGraw, McGraw Experimental Garden, Portland, Oregon.)

Eucalyptus globulus, the "blue gum", was one of first species introduced from Australia and one so largely planted for oil and gumwood furniture. (Photo by Larry L. McGraw, McGraw Experimental Garden, Portland, Oregon.)

ROPE-SCARRED
TREES *on Laurel Hill*

"God never made a mountain but he provided a place for man to go over or around it". Whether William K. Barlow actually believed this or was expressing hope and raising the spirits of the beleaguered immigrants is not known but it is a fact that he was a brave leader and brought his charges safely around the mountain to the Willamette Valley.

The earliest immigrants who came by wagon into Oregon ended the long trek at The Dalles Mission on the Columbia River. There they transferred their meager belongings to rafts and boats to complete the trip to Vancouver, Washington. Then they still had to go a few more miles either up the tributary Willamette or by wagon to Oregon City. From the mission the Columbia was a churning mass of hazards—rapids, falls and Indian attacks to which many of the pioneers had succumbed.

More or less prepared for this final ordeal those arriving at the mission in 1845 found a disheartening obstacle. There were no boats or rafts except a few priced out of reach. And all of these hard-pressed travelers were down to their last crumbs of food.

Out of this desperation one man stood tall. Born to lead, William Barlow proposed to the wagon masters that the trains make an attempt to strike out around the southeast shoulder of Mount Hood. His party would do that, he said. And most of the others saw some hope in the plan and agreed to go along.

In late September of that year a ragged procession of 7 wagons carrying 19 adults and several children with about 50 head of livestock headed south from The Dalles. At first the going was not much worse than it had been all the way west. Slopes were surmountable. Forests were of widely spaced ponderosa pine. Turning west at the foot of Mount Hood, the train passed over the Cascade summit, this range separating the arid eastern part of the state from the luxuriously forested western section receiving the bulk of northern Oregon's rainfall.

Now came the big troubles. Wagons had to be squeezed between closely spaced Douglas firs and the slopes became steeper. At the top of one hill, covered with native rhododendrons so prolific in rainy areas of these mountains, they found a seemingly impossible pitch. Even as desperate as the situation was the hardy wayfarers took note of these shrubs and mistook them for their laurels back home, the foliage being similar, and they named the terrifying drop "Laurel Hill".

William Barlow's appeal to the Almighty was aided by strong ropes carried by most of the wagons. The men made the big firs work for them now by securing the wagons one by one and lowering them with double hitches of rope around the trees, paying it out a little at a time. At each rope's length a new hitch was made on a lower tree until every wagon was safely down.

"Easy now! One foot at a time!" The late Colista Dowling, author, fine artist and Oregon history enthusiast, did this imaginative painting of wagons being lowered down Laurel Hill, with historical accuracy. In foreground are depicted some of rhododendrons, characteristic of area. (Painting by courtesy Oregon Historical Society publications.)

Down this rocky "chute" all wagons had to be lowered with restraint. Stump is one of trees used in snubbing-wagons down steep grade.

Scars made by restraining ropes. Note evidences of passing time—forest fires and natural decay. Many trees girdled by ropes died when natural flow of sap was cut off.

Stump at brink of steep slope shows clear evidence of scars caused by ropes. In foreground are small salal bushes, common undergrowth plant in Cascades, and manzanita with some berries showing.

Not-so-deeply scarred stump displays small rhododendron that gave hill its name—misnamed "laurel" by pioneers.

OLD DATE PALMS
and OLIVES of San Diego

In the summer of 1769 two Spanish packets arrived in San Diego Bay where they were to meet a land party from San Blas, Lower or Baja California. The object of the joint expedition was to establish military bases, or presidios, to retain the land for Spain which they thought was threatened by Russian encroachment from the north. Since no Spanish venture of this kind could be considered without sanction and cooperation of the Church, missions were to be set up near San Diego—the site selected being a point of land extending outwards toward Point Loma and the bay.

By the time of rendezvous the personnel of both parties was sadly depleted by scurvy. However, on July 16, 1769, Father Junipero Serra erected a brush hut and cross on the summit of Presidio Point and dedicated the first mission in California—San Diego de Alcala.

Some efforts were made at planting orchards and garden at the base of the hill but these were always near failure because of poor soil and long periods of drought. Fairly successful however was the planting of date seeds. A small group of the palms resulting survived many years.

Because of lack of water and many other difficulties (not the least being the proximity of Spanish soldiers to native women) the mission was moved to a site six miles up the San Diego River. Although the stream was seldom visible the water table could be reached by wells and later a dam was built farther up in the mountains. Traces of the historic mission dam remained for many years.

At this site the padres again set out an "orchard" more extensively planted with olives and cacti, as well as date palms. These trees survived until modern times when all were destroyed in the line of highways and condominiums.

Author's 1929 photo (*opposite top*) shows San Diego Mission before restoration, several of original date palms or offshoots of them still growing in front of building, at bottom, author's not too successful attempt with simple box camera in 1929 shows old date palms still standing. At base of trees is giant cactus hedge showing crop of fruits, originally one source of food supply for mission personnel.

Photo made in 1892 *(opposite)* shows two of original date palms, *Phoenix dactylifera*, planted by mission fathers to augment food supply. In 1769 on summit of Presidio Point were established first mission in California, first presidio and first place of white civilization in Alta California. Shortly after photo was made smaller palm was dug up and moved to Chicago's Columbian Exposition where it promptly died. The second barely survived until the late 1950s when it succumbed to rifle bullets and other vandalism. It was then cut down as safety measure. (Photo courtesy Historical Collection Title Insurance and Trust Co. San Diego).

Author's 1976 photo *(above)* of same area shows great contrasts. Presidio Point is entirely clothed in exotic trees of many kinds. At extreme right is portion of Marston Museum built by pioneer department store owner George Marston, dedicated July 16, 1929, on 160th anniversary of day Father Junipero Serra dedicated his first mission. In foreground are two young date palms near site of original ones. Feathery palm on horizon (center) is *Cocos plumosa* which actually bears inch-long coconuts, characteristically complete with three tiny eyes at tip.

If planting of date palms in 1769 could be called the beginning of the date industry in California, this grove of Deglet Noor date trees near Palm Desert *(above)* would represent ultimate development. Here in heated, irrigated desert are fabled requirements of date - "The date palm to succeed must have its roots in the water and its head in the fire."

One ornamental form of date *(above center)* is *Phoenix reclinata*. This graceful group flanks home facing ocean in Coronado, California.

Magnificent grove of one form of date, *Phoenix canariensis*, Canary Island palms growing close to Guasti Wineries near Santa Rosa, California.

Old photo *(above)* taken from near front steps of San Diego Mission showing old palms and fine grove of olive trees. Many of latter, while picturesquely gnarled, were in fine condition when author first saw them in 1925. Olive seeds were obtained from Mexico, along with the dates. While seedlings of many cultivated fruits prove inferior to standard, grafted varieties of the trees proved to be superior to European types. Seeds from the best were later the foundation of immense plantings in the great interior valleys of California, the "Mission" olive reigning supreme from about 1880. (Photo courtesy Historical Collection Title Insurance and Trust Co. San Diego).

1976 photo *(below)* made from same point shows some changes occurring over years. Comparatively young palm at right is *Phoenix canariensis*, closely related to date palms but with smaller, sparsely fleshed fruit.

OREGON'S
lost forest

"At this time of year," writes Ann Sullivan in Portland's *Oregonian,* December 12, 1974, "in the high desert of Central Oregon wind moves with peculiar moaning through the long needles of the marvelous trees of the Lost Forest.

"They are 40 miles from any other Ponderosa pine, this collection of pine and behemoth Western junipers, a climatological wonder in a desert that has no trees.

"There are roads from Christmas Valley, Brothers and Hampton, tortured with sand and rocks, by which one can reach these mysterious trees, but pity the motorist with a low oil pan.

"The entire 8,960-acre region has been declared the Lost Forest Research Natural Area by the Bureau of Land Management, which administers the forest. That means the trees will remain a natural wonder, living, growing and dying with no interference or help from man.

"This area long ago was an ocean or lake, and its gritty, wind-blown sands cover a hard pan of deposited sediment that moisture does not permeate. But the sands absorb and store with great efficiency rainfall that has averaged only 9.5 inches a year since 1901.

"That is half of what foresters say a yellow (Ponderosa) pine forest must have to grow and survive. The living has been tough for the tenacious trees, although some of the monstrous junipers have done so well they have produced mammoths dwarfing all others of known record. Hundreds of dead junipers, though, give evidence of the hard fight, for they are stark, naked ghosts against the blue sky, long dead, bleached by the hot sun of summer and cold of winter.

"The winds have dried them, and their trunks are furrowed in white splendor that has artists and photographers ecstatic.

"The Ponderosa which gives the forest its greatest mystery, also bear mute evidence of their difficulty. Branches seem to hang lower on the distinctive yellow-barked trunks and thicker. Young trees are thick and slow-growing, but there are quite a few of them.

"At this time of year, the ground is cracked with deep furrows from the dryness, and clusters of yellow rabbit brush and many dried desert weeds and flowers bend to the winds.

"The pines that have fallen have amazingly convoluted root systems, extraordinarily shallow, showing they did not go deep into the hard pan but spread widely to get every possible drop of moisture.

"The thick carpeting of old cones and needles makes tinder dry and scrunchy noise as one passes. The silence is eerie, for there are virtually no people, no major animals; only the quiet holes of burrowing creatures and migrating birds.

"Temperature drops precipitously when the red of sunset fades. The white ghosts of the junipers twist eerily everywhere in the pale moonlight. And again the wind whines, roughing through the long needles of the pines, no more lost but always persistent."

Oregon's high desert *(above)* is full of natural wonders, among them the almost unknown Lost Forest. Only recently came the answer to the mystery—how could the luxurious growth of ponderosa pine flourish in an area of much less rainfall than required for normal growth? View is of sandy road approaching Lost Forest in far distance. Juniper flanking road is typical of area, can survive on less moisture than pines (Photo Ann Sullivan, Portland).

Blowing sand scours signboard. Another year will see complete obliteration of sign. In background are ponderosa pines of Oregon's Lost Forest. More typical of high desert vegetation are rabbit brush (foreground center) and sage, *Artemisia* (right)—(Photo Ann Sullivan, Portland).

Lovely artist Martha Renfroe, Road's End, points out details of distinctive ponderosa needles, longer than those of any other pine native to Oregon. Another detail of identification is fact that they grow in clusters of three (Photo Ann Sullivan, Portland).

The
DISCOVERY
tree

"Walk the Sequoia woods at any time of year and you will say they are the most beautiful and majestic on earth. Beautiful and impressive contrasts meet you everywhere: The colors of tree and flower, rock and sky, light and shade, strength and frailty, endurance evanescence, tangles of supple hazel-bushes, tree-pillars about as rigid as granite domes, roses and violets, the smallest of the kind, blooming around the feet of the giants, and rugs of the lowly chamaebatia where the sunbeams fall."

John Muir,
The Mountains of California

Discovered in 1852? How could anybody miss it? A natural enough question in our present day awareness with the woods, the Sierra Nevada foothills crawling with tourists, rock hounds and snow mobiles. Yet back in the Gold Rush days very little was known of California and "Down East" seafarer Dowd was rightfully entitled to his shock when he first saw the tree, just as those who heard his story were entitled their unbelief.

In their natural beauty shaming great man made structures, the sequoias which grow in scattered groves along the western slope of the Sierra piedmont from Placer County south to the northern edges of Tulare County stand massive and tall in the field of western trees. These are the *Sequoia gigantea, (Sequoiadendron giganteum* say some authorities) and while they have greater girth, they are not as tall as their brothers growing in abundance on the northern California coast and across the line into Oregon, the *Sequoia sempervirens.* And there is another striking difference between these two giants.

The coastal tree readily regenerates itself, the stump of a cut tree often sending up ferny shoots in a ring that may grow into a tight clump of trees. This assures a continuance of the groves in some form. Big brother in the Sierra foothills has no such means of perpetuation. Once cut it is dead. Seedlings thrive but will not attain the size of many in the Calaveras grove for some 3,000 years.

The Baronoff Russians at Fort Ross, north of San Francisco, made early commercial use of the coastal redwoods, Spanish explorers noted their presence and the grandees in the Santa Cruz area cut them for use on their estates.

The *Sequoia gigantea* had the greater distinction of being "discovered". While the Miwoc and Washo Indians knew about them and in 1833 a party of trappers led by Capt. Bonneville, passed over the Sierra Nevada crest and through the groves. In spite of food shortages and fears of freezing to death one member of the

Most outstanding trees in Sequoia Grove were distinguished by naming them for prominent persons. Many decry this practice, believing it presumptious to attach names of mere mortals to these venerable monarchs. Yet a name seems better than a number for identification. This one was called Mark Twain Tree but it was cut down with the apparent intention of mounting an exhibit in American Museum of Natural History in New York and British Museum in London (C. C. Curtis photo from *Redwood Classic* by Ralph W. Andrews).

group, Zenas Leonard, made notes about the big trees in his diary which never came to public notice.

Early Spanish explorers noted the presence of the coastal redwoods. The first recorded sighting of them was in October, 1769, Gaspar de Portola and a small party sent in search of Monterey Bay to found a mission there saw the great trees and named them "palo colorado." The Spanish grandees cut them on their land grant estates. At Fort Ross, north of San Francisco the Baranoff Russians made commercial use of the redwoods, exporting posts and shingles to the Farallones and Sandwich Islands.

So out of the swarms of gold seekers in 1849 came the first news of these "fabulous forests." No one believed the first settlers who saw them, passing their reports off as something out of the "d.ts" or just plain "cock-and-bull" tales. But now enters Augustus T. Dowd, who in the spring of 1852, went hunting for deer or bear in the high country to feed the crews of the Union Water Co. which was building flumes to supply the construction camps above Murphys. Actually he was only one of a party sent out for the meat but he was the important one.

Cruising away from the others he sighted a bear and wounding it, followed the blood trail deeper into the woods. Almost at once he forgot the bear for there in front of his bugged-out eyes was a tree he could not believe ever existed. He was a seafaring man from Connecticut and used to trees he could put his arms around. Ten men couldn't stretch around this one. It was unbelievable and unbelievable was what the others in the party thought of his story when he ran back to tell them. They were more interested in getting something to eat rather than something to hug. They shrugged off Dowd's enthusiasm and shook their heads in sympathy for the poor man.

On his next day off Augustus returned to "his tree" with a long string and measuring its circumference, found it at more than 100 feet. But back at camp it was "unbelievable" again. "You might just as well have put that string around six trees." Only one man thought Dowd might have something, John De Lattre, who had some influence with the company. He accompanied a special party led by "the discoverer" to check out the story. After following a few false trails the men came face to face with the monster. Just how Augustus T. Dowd had his revenge is not known but it is to be presumed he was somewhat distinguished in camp and no doubt had two pieces of pie for supper.

It was inevitable that other giant trees would be located but the Dowd tree remained "King of the Forest". Yet to these construction men it was no monarch to hold them in silent reverence, to bow their heads under the mighty shaft reaching toward Heaven. There was gold in that great bole that some of the men had not found in the creek gravel. They formulated plans to fall the tree, saw and chop it into sections, ship it to New York to be reassembled and displayed at a handsome profit.

The perpetrators, being more familiar with picks, gold pans and carpenter tools than with timber falling gear and techniques, brought up pump augers and, 3-inch diameter drills, ordinarily used for making hollow wooden pipes. Attacking the old tree from all sides, boring holes for several days, the tree stood stalwart as ever. The holes were filled with blasting powder which was touched off. The tree still resisted. Further efforts were made with saws, axes and wedges. As the crew stopped to eat lunch a sharp breeze suddenly completed the heinous deed, the great bulk falling to earth with a crash that could be heard for miles.

A complete circle of 10-foot sections of bark was cut and numbered for reassembly in New York, a section of log removed to go with the shipment. The pieces were taken down the mountain by wagon and loaded on a river steamer for San Francisco. There the bark sections were set up to make a "salon", complete with fancy carpeting. Some 140 school children were admitted to the display, the throng "finding no inconvenience", as quoted in a local newspaper. Later a band played for 32 waltzing couples.

The display was then put aboard a vessel and shipped around The Horn to New York. The great P.T. Barnum himself took charge, meeting many difficulties in finding suitable space and setting up "the show". The opening finally came without crowds as the publicity appeared too early in view of the delays. Most of the people who did attend went away crying, "Fraud! There just ain't any tree that big!" Hoping to turn disaster to success the sections were to be crated and shipped to Paris where, it was hoped, the French might be more believing. Then a fire destroyed the exhibit parts and hopes of gold went glimmering with the charred remains of The Discovery Tree.

50 men stand around rim of Mark Twain stump. Note tools used in falling huge tree. Although two 10-foot crosscut saws were brazed together end to end combined length was not enough for efficiency. Exhibit section measured 16′ inside bark, this often 20″ to 30″ thick (C. C. Curtis photo from *Redwood Classic* by Ralph W. Andrews).

Stump of Discovery Tree was smoothed off and made into dance floor in July 1856. 1861 lithograph by Edward Vischer is captioned "The Stump and Tree of the Mammoth Tree of Calaveras". Term Discovery Tree came into use later (Photo reproduced courtesy *The Enduring Giants* by Joseph H. Engebreck Jr. California Dept. Parks and Recreation).

Side street in now quiet Murphys, among most historic of California's gold camps. Note characteristic iron shutters. It was here brothers John and Daniel Murphy discovered gold and Union Water Co. had headquarters. An employee, sent to higher elevations to hunt game for camp food discovered Calaveras Grove of Big Trees.

At left is Mitchler Hotel still appearing much like it did when built in 1856. Impressive names are listed on old registers—Horatio Alger, Jr., Charles Bolton (Black Bart), Thomas Lipton, Ulysses S. Grant, Henry Ward Beecher, John Jacob Astor Jr., John Pierpont Morgan and Will Rogers who made a movie here in 1934 (Florin photo from his *Ghost Town Album*).

Sequoia grave of Captain Daniel Wright *(above left)*. Arriving in Oregon from east in 1849 he heard clarion cry, "Gold in California!" and moved south to make name and fortune in gold fields of Sierra Nevada. With other immigrants who were farmers at heart, Wright pocketed seeds so voluminously produced by giant sequoias growing nearby. Home after little success he planted some of his seeds, saw them sprout to sapling size. But Wright could only nurture tiny trees for short while. He was killed in fall from building where he was working and was buried in Portland's old Lone Fir Cemetery in 1873. His grieving wife saw to it that in death he would be near his trees from California. Four tiny sequoias were planted on grave, one at each corner.

Sequoia seeds are exceedingly fine - 5,600 to ounce and a seedling that might grow to 300' is an inch tall once tiny husk is shed.

General Grant Tree in Grant Grove *(above center)* is 267' tall with maximum circumference of 40.3'. At 200' above earth diameter is 12'.

Designated as National Shrine, General Grant Tree presides above special services at high noon each Christmas day (Uncredited photo from New Standard Encyclopedia 1940 edition).

Extremely contrasty light *(above right)* nevertheless reveals deeply furrowed bark of giant redwood in South Grove section of Calaveras Trees. Author's head in lower left corner gives scale.

By 1861 private owners Sperry and Perry had built fancy pavilion over Discovery Stump and new hotel constructed. Fountain is surrounded by clipped greensward, in this fanciful drawing by Edward Vischer (opposite page bottom). Romantic touch is string of camels although some did pass through grove in 1861 (Reproduced courtesy *The Enduring Giants* by Joseph Engebreck Jr. California Dept. Parks and Recreation).

Mark Twain Tree falls to sudden death (C. C. Curtis photo from *Redwood Classic* by Ralph W. Andrews).

In 1852 this was largest and most nearly perfect giant sequoia in the North Grove, also apparently fastest growing. Careful study of tree's annual growth rings revealed it was "only" about 1,300 years old. All of later annual rings were about ½" thick. If tree had continued to grow at this phenomenal rate it would by now have added 5' of thickness to its trunk and would probably be largest giant sequoia - largest living thing—in world.

Casey Kendall of Portland *(above center)* does a modern teenage step on Discovery Stump where 32 persons waltzed in 1856. Note Kendall wears hair (in 1976) exactly as men did 120 years ago.

Vigorous young grove *(above right)* in Portland's Eastmoreland Golf Course area shows structure and habit better than mature veterans which would dwarf such structures as Campanile on University of California campus at Berkeley, Statue of Liberty or National Capitol Dome.

Woodpecker "Storehouse". Up to 100′ each redwood is riddled with work of California woodpeckers which find soft, thick bark ideal for storing acorns. Hoarded nuts seem not to be much used, many decayed with age.

This occurs in small grove within town limits of old mining camp in Sierra piedmont, North San Juan, which offers many attractions among historic buildings, brick-fronted, iron-shuttered and frilled with iron grill work. Not always noticed are fascinating stones in old cemetery and sequoias growing within its iron fences. These fine trees are very near northern limit of their range and in author's experience are only sequoias growing within a town limit even though town is near ghost.

General Sherman Tree discovered by James Wolverton Aug. 7, 1879 is largest living thing in world. Height in 1930 was 272.4', base circumference 101.6', age between 3,000 and 4,000 years. Sequoias theoretically go on living until fire, storms, lightning or man bring life to end. (Photo California Historical Society, San Francisco).

Typical foliage of Giant Sequoia is steely gray green, sharp and raspy to touch. Seed cones are not borne until tree is several hundred years old. Seeds have been distributed to all parts of temperate world, especially to England where they were originally named *Wellingtonia.*

STADTER

buried forest

"The phenomenon of greatest interest," wrote Carl Price Richards in *Mazama Annual,* dated December, 1931, "which has been investigated by the Research Committee this season is the Stadter Buried Forest on the west side of Mount Hood at elevation 6200. In July, 1926, when Judge Fred W. Stadter was exploring in the Paradise Park district, he saw on the far side of a canyon what appeared to be large tree trunks protruding from the canyon wall some distance below its rim. There was no opportunity then to cross the canyon, so a closer investigation had to be deferred to a future occasion.

It was not until late in the season of 1930 that another visit was made in an endeavor to get close to this feature. The approach was from Paradise Park and an attempt made to get to the far side of the canyon by climbing to its upper reaches. Rough terrain and insufficient time defeated the attempt.

Last July a party of three set out to reach this buried forest. They bivouaced at Camp Blossom and, starting early, climbed to Illumination Rock. From there they followed a spur of the mountain which leads down directly to the ridge, forming the north side of the canyon where the trees are located. The trip, therefore, involved a climb of 3200 feet to elevation 9000, then a descent to 6200, followed by a return over the same route.

The party reached the place about mid-day and spent some time in cutting a sample of the wood, taking photographs and generally investigating the unique and interesting feature. Its importance from a scientific standpoint in throwing light upon the geological history of the mountain was obvious, so it was decided to request Dr. Edwin T. Hodge, Professor of Geology at the University of Oregon, and a member of our Research Committee, to let us have a report concerning it. Dr. Hodge readily agreed and later submitted an account, reproduced in full in these pages, giving a graphic description of what is now to be seen and an analysis of the series of probable events and their causes which led to these trees becoming buried in this place:"

Early in July, 1926, Judge Fred W. Stadter of Portland discovered a buried forest on the slopes of Mount Hood. The buried forest lies on the south side of the spur which separates Reid from Zig-Zag Glacier, called Illumination Spur. The entombed trees lie on the north side of the north fork of the south fork of Sandy River at an elevation of 6200 feet. The occurrence of the ancient forest is very significant in deciphering the history of the little-known southwest side of Mount

Article by Dr. Edwin T. Hodge, professor of geology, University of Oregon, appeared in Mazama Annual, publication of Mazamas, Portland, Oregon, mountain climbing group, December, 1931.

Hood. Judge Stadter's discovery is to be ranked as one of the most significant in the investigation of Mount Hood. The writer is very familiar with the region in which the fossil forest occurs, having examined it in 1926 and 1927, though I regret that upon neither occasion was I fortunate enough to discover these ancient trees. This report is based upon my own observation, the discussion of Judge Stadter, the excellent photographs of C.P. Richards and upon the report of Richard Bogue, who was sent to the area specifically to investigate the buried trees.

The Stadter Buried Forest lies beneath and on a mass of glacial till which in turn lies on an andesite lava flow. The complete section exposed by a deep V-shaped canyon cut by the fork of the Sandy River, exposes andesite flows with interbedded sediments below and glacial till above.

The Sandy River has cut a canyon about 300 feet deep in these beds. Falls occur where it cuts over the andesite flows, one being just below the buried forest and another upstream at 6700 feet elevation. The two falls are determined by the two andesite flows which are exposed in the valley below the fossil forest. The fossil forest lies about 40 feet above the topmost andesite lava flow.

The exhumed portion of the ancient forest is only a part of what apparently is a still larger buried mass. Only about 60 feet of the forest is exposed; the larger mass of trees is covered by 25 to 30 feet of debris.

The individual trees within the exposed mass lie almost north and south, that is, parallel to the north side of the north lobe of Zig-Zag Glacier, and hence are part of a former lateral moraine. The bark is entirely removed from the trees, and they are scarred, battered, splintered and twisted. Mr. Bogue counted eleven trees which were prostrated in a layer as one would get if a forest were overridden. Their diameter is from 1 to 3 feet.

The trees do not lie on the soil on which they grew, not upon any soil. Apparently that soil is now mixed with the over and underlying glacial till. This glacial till may be traced eastwards to Zig-Zag Glacier.

There are no trees nor even shrubs near the buried forest. In fact the only vegetation in the vicinity is moss growing on the west side of the spur on which the trees occur. Five hundred feet lower on the mountainside is a gallery forest.

The evidence and some speculative conclusions will, as far as possible be stated in their historical sequence.

1. Illumination Rock, Crater Rock and Steel's Cliff are parts of the last crater of Mount Hood. During or shortly after the time of activity of this crater, trees grew on the slopes of Mount Hood at an elevation of about 7000 feet. The trees did not cling to the mountain slopes because of decayed soil, but sank their roots into the fresh, pervious, soft volcanic debris on its slopes. The conditions controlling the existence of vegetation on a mountain slope are sun exposure, moisture, wind direction and velocity and temperature. Sun exposure, wind direction and velocity we may conclude have been nearly uniform for a period of time longer than we here are considering. The other two factors are subject to speculation. If no glacier were present the mean average temperature would have been higher and the available moisture less. This conclusion derives factors that mutually counter each other. If however, we add that a slightly active crater would have by reason of the steam ejected, bathed the mountain slopes with many fog clouds and occasionally a rain. Both the fog and rain would have been warm. The warm rains resulting from vulcanism must have melted the glaciers and caused them to contract so that they all disappeared or occupied but a small area. The absence of glaciers and the presence of an active crater produced a condition favorable to a stand of trees at a higher elevation than at present.

An alternate to the above theory is a climatic change that permitted the forest to climb higher than at present on Mount Hood.

2. When vulcanism ceased, the warm moist blankets of fog disappeared and the warm rains ceased. After that the usual winter cold rains or snow-fall on Mount Hood produced snow-fields which were too large to melt during summers. Hence, annual residues of snow accumulated and in time were compacted and transformed into glaciers. The glaciers grew headward and moved down the mountain side. Growing headward, the Zig-Zag and White River Glaciers cut into the sides of the crater; cut through the crater wall and into the crater pit where now they are still at work tearing down the north and east walls—that is, the top of Mount Hood.

The downward movement of Zig-Zag Glacier advanced upon the helpless forest. The high mass of ice moved against, froze around, and then buried within itself the trees of the former rain-forest. The ice-bound trees were twisted and wrenched in the ice which moved foot by foot down the mountain side. The boulders and other debris which Zig-Zag Glacier had picked up on its march were used to further batter and gouge the trees.

The Zig-Zag Glacier moved, not to the edge of the present forest, but far beyond. It moved down Zig-Zag Canyon to Salmon River and down Salmon River to just beyond Salmon postoffice. Here it left a terminal moraine. We know this because the existing forest stands on ground that was eroded after the glacier's retreat. This moraine was the combined work of Sandy, Reid and Zig-Zag Glaciers.

But where is the rest of the forest that might have been overwhelmed by such a glacial advance? The answer is: there was no forest present; only a rain forest stood on Mount Hood; the general area was not forested. If the aridity was such that no glacier existed on Mount Hood, then perhaps it was such that no forest existed on the western lava and ash-covered slopes of Mount Hood. At least our present investigation shows that no large amount of fossil wood is preserved in the moraines. Perhaps the moraines at Salmon were made during an earlier glacial stage and, if so, then we must postulate the advance of Zig-Zag Glacier to some lesser distance. Evidence on this point is given several paragraphs below.

From the farthest advanced glacial stand, wherever that might have been, it then retreated, leaving below its melting front a great amount of glacial till. Thus some thirty to forty feet of glacial till entomb the forest. Evidently the buried mantle was laid not gently on the mangled trees, but roughly and as an after-event. Evidently the trees were killed, bruised and overridden and for a long time lay buried beneath the ice. They were not buried where they stood and died, but were dragged a long distance, perhaps several thousand feet down the mountain side. This is proven by the absence of soil on the lava on which the trees lie and by their mutilated condition when exhumed. The trees and their soil apparently were scraped away and carried, the soil mixed with the glacial till, to the burying ground.

Thus the trees lie on glacial till deposited during the advance and are buried beneath a pall of glacial till deposited when the glacier retreated.

After the Zig-Zag Glacier had retreated, waters derived from the melting glacier washed sand and gravel down the slopes and over the moraine.

Zig-Zag Glacier has continued to retreat up to and above 7600 feet elevation. Does not the fossil forest tell a story of a long continued glacial retreat? How long ago was the recession begun? The answer is seen in the deep 300-foot V-shaped canyons cut through glacial-wash moraine, and the lava flows. These canyons are, geologically, very young. They are so young that no sane man attempts to climb their slopes. They are so young and so steep that every wandering breeze dislodges pebbles and pebbles shake loose boulders and all start landslides down their walls. Several of my men have been thrilled, fortunately none injured, by attempting to follow down the bottom of one of these valleys. Young as these canyons are geologically speaking, it took a long time for the waters to cut through the thick lava flows. This took time despite the fact that the running waters moved over a steep slope and were abundantly supplied with cutting tools.

If we assume that the new forest began its hesitating advance soon after the glacier's retreat we can, perhaps, get a clear or even positive evidence of the time required. The new forest certainly did not cover the slope till after most of the young valleys had been well cut. If the forest formed before the valleys were carved, then we should find trees undermined by the streams. However, the forests probably started to climb the mountain slopes soon after the streams began cutting into the glacio-fluvial cover on which the trees stand. If this conclusion be true, then we may hope to find some venerable tree still living or perhaps the body of one long since fallen, yet preserved, that started growing soon after the retreat of Zig-Zag Glacier. The annual rings of this tree compared with some of the living trees would tell us exactly when Zig-Zag Glacier started its retreat.

Turning now to another possibility, to-wit, that Zig-Zag Glacier did not advance far down the slopes of Mount Hood and permitted a part of the rain forest to stand, then we would be in great luck. Such luck, however is more than I expect since such evidence as we have indicates the absence of a forest. We should, however, leave no possibility untested, hence I recommend that the research committee of the Mazamas begin the collection of tree sections for the purpose of comparison and the building up of a chronological scale. It will be hoped that by that method we shall find an ancient tree whose rings correspond with the outermost ring of the Stadter Buried Forest. If such be found we shall know exactly how long ago the forest lived. I venture the guess that its age will be numbered in thousands of years. The fact that the wood of the fossil is not decayed does not prove that it might not be 5000 years old.

Stratum (opposite top) in glacial moraine below Illumination Rock and above Paradise Park on Mount Hood contains many long dead trees, remnants of "Stadter Buried Forest". On exposure trees readily crumble although remaining intact for thousands of years while buried in glacial till. (Photo Donald Onthank, honorary member and past president of Mazamas, Portland, Oregon, climbing organization).

Some remnants of buried trees (opposite bottom) are more than 3' in diameter, far larger than tiny alpine specimens now growing at much lower altitudes. Theory is, in eons past, warmer climate prevailed allowing much higher timber line than at present. Later lowering of growth limits killed trees which were eventually undermined and buried in glacier ice. Inexorable downward progress of glacier and moraine melted ice near surface. Presence a few feet down in gravel is here betrayed by seepage (dark area left of center). Note two lava "bombs" beside stump. (Photo Donald Onthank).

Prehistoric trees *(left)* long buried in glacial moraines, other than those first discovered by Judge Stadter, have long been noted by author. Here are plainly seen several specimens protruding from edge of White River Glacier moraine, (shown lower right of center). Illumination Rock is first large projection encountered on long south slope (at left). Actually a remnant of eroded south center rim, it lies immediately above site of Stadter Buried Forest. More nearly preserved north section of crater rim is seen here curving around Crater Rock, solidified neck of molten lava flow when volcano was active.

Author stands at foot of Illumination Rock to photograph (center) awesome upper ice fall on Reid Glacier. In 1901 Harry Fielding Reid, of John Hopkins University, made extensive explorations on glaciers of Mount Hood and other peaks. Deep crevasses here are caused by fracturing ice stream as it moves down steep slope and represent one of most dangerous spots for climbers. Area is near of slightly above level where conjecture places possible growth of large trees later buried in glacier ice, then carried to lower levels in glacier's slow descent.

Ice and morainal gravels in canyon immediately below brink shown here (right) here undermined these trees, killing by removal of half the sandy soil supporting them. Stream of descending ice at left is White River Glacier. From it springs White River. Rushing eastward, turgid rapids were serious impediment to those wagon trains electing newer route around Mount Hood rather than even more dangerous voyage down rapids of Columbia River.

Splendid Tree of Heaven grows one block from author's home in Portland. Shown here in full bloom, apparent flowers are actually clusters of seeds, each single one bearing brilliant orange-red pair of wings.

TREE of HEAVEN

The gold rush to the Sierra foothills in the 1850s and 60s created vast changes in the lives of thousands and in a smaller way the waves of immigration made many changes in plant life, including some trees. Prospectors returning to their homes often planted sequoia seeds picked up in such native groves as the Calaveras, a few miles above Angel's Camp. Thousands of Chinese, imported to work on the railroads or attracted to the same gold fields, carried with them a bit of nostalgia, seeds of their classic temple trees—"Trees of Heaven". These soon became well established in gold camps and readily spread to other areas not too cold for them.

Gardeners' approval of the trees to cultivated areas is not unanimous. Some regard the tree as extremely desirable because it will withstand any amount of smoke and pollution, and when injured or blown down will rapidly regenerate itself, even from root cuttings. Often in cities where introduced, then neglected, seedlings will spring up through cracks in pavements and flourish there for tropical effect. It casts a sparse shade favorable to most ornamental flowers.

Others regard the Tree of Heaven as an obnoxious weed, party because of its very persistence or because the leaves exude a fetid odor as do the flowers.

Generally speaking, the Tree of Heaven, *Ailanthus altissima,* because of its height, or *glanulosa* because of two smelly glands at the base of the compound leaves, should not be planted in cramped or windy areas but certainly makes a superb showing where rapid growth is desired.

Detail of fruits and leaf of Tree of Heaven. Compound leaves are similar to those of Juglans (hickories, black walnuts etc), latter lacking in basal glands characteristic of *Ailanthus*.

WORLD'S LARGEST FIR

Washington and Oregon have similar terrains, commercial and social conditions with other problems common to both. They maintain a stately friendship while harboring some envies and jealousies however softened by good humor. They both have great stands of Douglas fir and have vied for years as to which state can boast of the biggest one. Let Ann Sullivan, with her Irish name, tell the story of Finnegan's fir, with its Irish name. It appeared in the Portland *Oregonian* in June, 1975.

"The record of the world's largest Douglas fir tree has been returned to Oregon after a 13-year reign of the famed Queets tree on the Olympic Peninsula. The new one is near Coos Bay and is named Finnegan fir.

"The Queets tree, which had title for many years originally under an inflated measurement, lost the title to Oregon once before, in 1962, only to regain it when the Clatsop fir near the Cannon Beach-Seaside Junction on Klootchey Creek was weakened by the Columbus Day storm and blew down in a second storm a month later.

"Oregon's new champion, officially given the title by the American Forestry Association, wins it by a complicated system of points on diameter, height and crown spread.

"The Queets tree was 14 feet, 5 inches in diameter and was 221 feet tall, but it had a broken top, victim of a lightning bolt years ago.

"So did the Clatsop fir, which was 200 feet high, but it was 15.48 feet in diameter at 4½ feet above average ground measurement. The Clatsop fir had more taper to its trunk, and the Queets tree a thicker average stalk, although not thicker at the bottom. Finnegan fir, its top intact, is 102 feet taller than Clatsop and 81 feet taller than Queets.

"Oregon's new champion is 13 feet, 3½ inches in diameter, is 302 feet tall, with a crown diameter of 67 feet. Its tremendous height gives it an impressive bearing above a mixed undergrowth of hemlock and cedar, as well as an average of 51,000 board feet of lumber up to its 18-inch top. That would make 17 sixteen-foot logs.

Study of Tree of Heaven *(opposite top)* shows detail of bark with light colored lines running vertically. This specimen is direct descendant of those brought by Chinese miners to California gold camps, still flourishing among picturesque ruins of Campo Seco. Bottom, Tree of Heaven in winter garb and late afternoon light in Old Shasta, gold camp at edge of California's Trinity Mountains.

"That is a very tall tree to get into one picture", says Ann Sullivan, well known Portland *Oregonian* medical writer who shows talent here as perservering photographer. She adds, "even with good equipment. I climbed up the steep facing hill, pushed through typical underbrush, fortunately aided by pushes from behind." Her friend (figure in white raincoat) stands at base to give scale to 302-foot Finnegan's fir. (Photo by Ann Sullivan, Portland *Oregonia*.)

"The Coos Bay giant stands on a slope of an unnamed creek flowing a mile and a half before it reaches the east fork of the Coquille River. It is in the Burnt Mountain Resource Area, Coos Bay District, Bureau of Land Management. It can be reached by a short walk from a graveled road.

"Total points achieved by the Finnegan fir is 810, compared to 781 for the Queets fir. The Coos Bay tree will be named for its discoverer, Lance Finnegan, Coos Bay, BLM timber management specialist, who found it about four years ago.

"'My reaction was wow, it's a big tree,' said Finnegan. He found it on a 70 per cent slope at an elevation of 2,000 feet, near a ridgetop, in a 25-acre grove of large trees north of the historic Coos Bay Wagon Road. Finnegan said old growth, or virgin, firs are numerous, with several having a diameter of better than eight feet. The Finnegan fir is between 700 and 1,000 years old, about the same as the Clatsop and Queets firs, according to the BLM.

"BLM's Coos Bay District Manager Ed Stauber said the area has been administratively removed from the district's timber production base. Stauber said BLM has a policy of protecting unique stands of trees.

"Finnegan entered the tree in a recent contest sponsored by Albert Wiesendanger of the Keep Oregon Green Association. He will receive a $100 reward."

Ann Sullivan, Lance Finnegan, Coos Bay and all responsible citizens of Oregon had their day of rejoicing but it came to a sad end on November 10, 1975 amid wailings and gnashing of teeth. Now let an *Oregon Journal* writer tell that story. It appeared on November 18, 1975, headlined:

VIOLENT FALL OF A CHAMP

"Al Wiesendanger, the ageless and usually cheerful secretary of the Keep Oregon Green Association, (KOG) was a bit downcast last week.

"The reason? Oregon has again lost the Douglas fir tree championship after having held it all too short a time.

"Violent winds felled the 302-foot giant, Finnegan's fir, located on Bureau of Land Management lands in a remote area between Coos Bay and Roseburg. While the tree had been discovered in 1971 by Lance Finnegan, BLM forester, it had been certified only recently by the American Forestry Association as being larger than the Queets fir in Washington's Olympic National Park.

"Size is determined by a point system based on diameter, height and crown spread. The Queets fir, which lost its top to a lightning strike, is a "mere" 221 feet tall but much thicker. Its dimensions make it less vulnerable to powerful winds.

"This will be the second time the Queets tree has regained the title. In November, 1962, a giant fir on Crown-Zellerbach lands in Clatsop County was blown down after having survived the region's worst storm in recent memory on Oct. 12 of that year. It had been judged the nation's champ not long before that, wrestling the title from the Washington tree.

"Finnegan's fir was estimated to have been 700 to 1,000 years old. It was already a giant at the time of Columbus' arrival in the New World. Huge firs are scarcer than they used to be, but Oregon has some known to be taller than Finnegan's though not as big over all.

"Finding a new champ is not out of the question. Al Wiesendanger will be pushing the search."

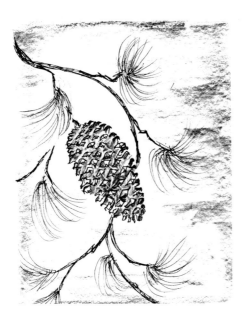

Giant fir measures 13 feet, 3½ inches in diameter, 491 inches in circumference. Standing proudly in front of world's largest Douglas fir is its discoverer, Lance Finnegan, Bureau of Land Management forester in Coos Bay, Oregon, district. At right, Enid Ruble (Photo by Ann Sullivan, Portland *Oregonian*).

Mary Charlotte's

LILAC TREE

After five moves it's still lilac time on the Foster "homestead" at Eagle Creek, Oregon.

State of Mainers, Philip and Mary Foster (Mary Charlotte Pettygrove, sister of a Portland founder) came to the Oregon country by sea in 1842. During the first four years Philip was engaged in the mercantile business in Oregon City.

Deciding that farming was more to his taste he took out a homestead at Eagle Creek a few miles east of Oregon City, located on what would become the Oregon Trail for those who did not depart from it at The Dalles to take the hazardous voyage through the rapids of the Columbia River on rafts.

One October day in 1845 Foster and sons Frank and George, aged six and eight were at work building a grist mill on Goose Creek. Straying from the job the boys came running back reporting they saw two strange white men in the woods. The men proved to be Samuel Barlow and William Rector who were the first party of immigrants to attempt a route around the south side of Mount Hood. Stranded at the brink of a slope too steep to descend by wagon, they fought their way on foot for six days through snowy, wet woods, and were nearly exhausted and starved. Foster saw to their immediate wants, helped them on to Oregon City where a party was formed to go to the aid of the miserable group still camping and six miles south of the summit.

This human effort initiated a unique operation to care for what soon grew to be a flood of pioneers arriving almost daily the next year.

Foster joined with Barlow to build a crude road around the south side of Mount Hood (originally called Mount Hood Road, later Barlow Road) and set up an establishment on his farm—log stables and corrals for animals, temporary shelters for immigrants. He built a large store (the stone steps of which still remain) and a warehouse. His first home was a log cabin, followed by a larger one, then in 1883 he built the frame building still standing on the site.

The lilacs? Mary Foster brought two small lilac trees, purple and white, and some moss roses, all the way from Maine, planting them immediately on her arrival at Oregon City. The purple one is the oldest and largest in the state.

Purple lilac, oldest and largest in Oregon, possibly the West, survived five moves after ocean voyage from Maine in 1843 and has been growing in this spot since 1883 when last Foster home (in background) was built. Following nature of ungrafted lilacs, this one sent up shoots around itself, then circle of shoots around cluster, then another until present group is more than 100 feet around. Original, no doubt much taller than survivors shown here, is dead.

Multiple trunks of ancient lilac, survivor of pair brought from Maine, lie on ground in center of thicket of younger trees.

Pink moss rose shown here is from author's garden, that at Foster home not in bloom when other photos were made. Other cuttings are being cared for by Clackamas County Historical Society.

LAVA CAST FOREST

Away back there, some 6,000 years ago, Oregon's Mount Newberry erupted or simply collapsed in a violent volcanic spasm. Activity did not stop with the cataclysm but as vents and cracks opened up molten lava continued to flow, the more heated and fluid freshets totally consuming all trees in its path. Slightly cooler flows enveloped living trees whose cool sapwood partially reduced and solidified the surrounding lava, the remaining, still hot, liquid material flowing on.

However the affected trees won only a little time, soon succumbing to extensive heat damage. As time went on the wood rotted completely away, leaving remarkably realistic casts. Varieties of trees so preserved are hard to identify but present day specimens are composed mostly of ponderosa and smaller lodgepole pines.

Although long known the Lava Cast Forest was almost inaccessible because of sandy, rough and steep roads when the author first tried to reach it. Rather recently the road has been much improved although it is still not paved—an easy 8 miles with some grades, exiting east from a well marked point on US 97, a few miles south of Bend. There is a large rest area at the site and a paved trail circling the area, merciful to feet and shoes as an alternative to walking on sharp lava rocks.

Good example of vertical cast. Clearly shown *(opposite top)* is thickness of shell once encasing living tree. This one had to be a ponderosa, lodgepoles not reaching this size.

Cream-colored specimen of lava rock flows from Newberry crater*(opposite bottom)* continued over long periods of time, each new flow likely differing in type and color from one previous. Other rocks are black (preponderating) and reddish. State of Oregon has quarried much road material from old cinder cones made up of latter type, causing many roads in eastern areas to gleam brightly red. All lava fragments are rough with many sharp protuberances making the shortest trek across a lava field ruinous to shoes.

Living trees and many dead ones *(above)* show
evidence of severe struggle to survive. This
copse of ponderosa pine seems still to writhe
though long since having given up battle.

View *(opposite top)* looks across lava flow from
near center. Pines now growing on field are few,
assuming bonsai aspect, tortured by rocky
terrain and lack of water, most precipitation
quickly draining out of sight, Bottom, not all
tree casts are standing, some felled by lava flow
and cased where they lay. Some are 50 feet long.
Author's dog eagerly explored each of these but
found no wild animals. Note dead pine that
reached good size before dying from austere
growing conditions.

Giant Juniper, *Juniperus Occidentalis*, is not quite champion of all junipers, that being southeast a few miles. This specimen grows near the route taken by one splinter group of Lost Wagon Train, could well have marked and sheltered one encampment. Water for stock and humans was completely lacking here as well as along much of route. Western juniper, as it is commonly called, has many other names—Western red cedar (name "cedar" being loosely used for many fine-foliaged, resinous trees) and Sierra juniper. Spaces between branches are short, wood knotty and tough, useless for lumber but so durable it provides most of fence posts in areas where plentiful. Lost Wagon Train party used trees as drags for wagons on steep hills. Some so used still exist, serve to help mark tortuous route taken.

DESERT CEDARS

"Anyone guilty of open adultery will be punished by 49 lashes on the bare back". This was one of a long list of strict rules laid down in an attempt to keep law and order during the tribulations of what later became known as the Lost Wagon Train of 1843. The train, originally traveling along conventional Oregon Trail routes was diverted into the high desert area of eastern Oregon by the persuasions of guide Stephen Meek. For a price, he said, he could lead the train on a much shorter route, a short cut to save many miles of travel. Instead he lost the way, the immigrants suffering many hardships and deaths.

Somewhere across the plain the party camped at a watering place where children picked up golden nuggets, placed them in a blue bucket which rode the remaining miles under a wagon. The "Blue Bucket Mine" has never been positively found but the legend refuses to die.

Various diaries and journals left by survivors of the Lost Wagon Train mention the welcome, although scanty shade offered by the "desert cedars" along the way, particularly in the area of the worst despair and thirst, east of Bend, south of Maury Mountains.

After a crossing of the Deschutes River, requiring a three weeks camp at Buck Hollow, bedraggled remnants of the train ascended Tygh Ridge and finally gained their temporary goal, the mission at The Dalles.

Bark of Western Juniper can be mistaken for no other tree. Deeply furrowed and fluted, connected by diagonal, firmly anchored strands, it seems wrinkled like Methuselah and indeed trees may reach age of 1,000 years.

Fine specimen of Western juniper shelters unofficial postoffice in days when tiny Grandview, (near Culver) Oregon, was touted by greedy developers. Eager land buyers, duped into giving up meager funds for plots of land for home place with promise of high resale values, were soon driven out by constant drouth.

"Utah Juniper", *(opposite) Juniperus Osteosperma*, is native to Great Basin, generally spreading to eastern slopes of Sierra Nevada, Panamints and contiguous ranges.

Madronas on Magnolia Point - trees mistaken by early arrivals to Puget Sound from southern states where magnolias are abundant. Foliage of both trees is superficially similar. Snowy peaks of Olympic Range shown in background.

MADRONAS
and MANZANITAS

It is easy to imagine the homesickness experienced by early immigrants from the East and South to the Pacific Coast after long trips across the plains, around Cape Horn or traversing Isthmus of Panama between two ocean voyages. Remembering "home" so vividly and being tree conscious, they made natural mistakes in likening trees and plants they found in this strange new world to the ones they were familiar with.

This was the case of one party rounding a point on the shore of Puget Sound. At the sight of exotic madronas with their glossy, leathery leaves similar to those of the magnolia of the deep South, they named the promontory "Magnolia Point".

The madrona, *Arbutus menziesii,* is a strictly western tree. It ranges from the coastal regions of British Columbia, along the shores of Puget Sound, south through Oregon's coastal range and heavily forested section of southern Oregon. They are found along California's coast and near San Diego extend back to the Lagunas and Cuyamacas, thence northward into the gold country in the Sierra Nevada. Author-naturalist Donald Culross Peattie, in his *Natural History of Western Trees,* writes of conspicuous trees associated with the madronas— California black oaks, splendid tan oaks, giant redwoods, adding, "Even in such distinguished arboreal company it outshines them all."

The madrona seems invariably to be in perfect health, seldom a broken down or diseased specimen ever seen. Where conditions are favorable to its growth it easily and commonly attains heights of 50 feet or more. One growing in a remote region of Humboldt County in northern California is called the "Council Madrono", and measures 75 feet tall with a crown spread of 99 feet. Its girth, 16 inches from the ground, is over 24 feet. Donald Culross Peattie notes the tree grows in an isolated area without close neighbors and gives the impression of a massive oak because of its spread and size. It was considered exceptional enough by Indians to serve as a focal point, a meeting place for tribal pow wows.

Considered here with the madronas are the manzanitas, *Archtostaphylos,* closely related (through the Ericas, both having characteristic urn-shaped flowers). Manzanita are often excluded from works dealing strictly with "trees", and truly is most often seen as a shrub but does attain tree status in favored locations, as shown in accompanying photos. As a crooked-stemmed shrub, tortured into twisted shapes, the deep, red-stemmed manzanita plant has been favored by those constructing "money", "candy" or imitation Ming trees. Its fruits are small red berries similar to tiny apples, hence the Spanish name manzanita (little apple).

No "parlor ivy" this but a stangling monster. Madrona is being slowly choked to death by rambling, tightly clinging vine. Clearly visible are past attempts to cut lower life lines of upper parts, efforts thwarted by unique ability of some plants to "self graft". At points where vines cross each other and subject to slight rubbing, scraping movements by winds, cambium layers can join, eventually allowing sap transfer nourishment from one vine to another. Thus an old vine may be severed at base but continue to draw sustenance from neighbor. In center, Jacksonville Cemetery seems fitting place for this example of madrona patient that died in spite of valiant efforts to save it.

Almost continually exfoliating trunks of older madronas reveal great beauty in under bark, at first tender chartreuse, turning to coppery red, both colors present at various places. Slightest touch dislodges frail, brittle flakes.

Exceptionally majestic group of madronas grow in historic old Jacksonville, Oregon, cemetery. Shown here *(above left)* is characteristic habit of bark to shed from upper reaches, often persistently clinging in scattered shreds but here falling cleanly. Ground is always thickly littered with crisp bark fragments and leaves falling after long season of growth. No one walks silently in a grove of madronas.

Glossy, leathery foliage of madronas hangs on tree for long periods to make it evergreen. In spring pink urn-shaped blossoms give way to brilliant orange berries, reluctant to drop. In October fruit is edible, was an important element in lives of Indians who seemed to tolerate laxative effects more than white man. Close relative to madrona is strawberry tree, another *Arbutus*, with inch-sized red fruits, more tasty and less drastic in effects to digestive system. Strawberry tree is less hardy than larger relative, is often winter damaged in Pacific Northwest.

Graceful young tree, *(above center) Magnolia soulangeana* is established in author's garden. Exposure by flash separates it from bamboo background.

Manzanitas usually thought of as shrubs grow here as small trees. Relationships to madronas, not always evident, is shown *(above right)* in flaking bits of bark being shed near base. Location is in Jewish section of Jacksonville, Oregon, Cemetery.

Possibly record height has been achieved by this group of manzanitas, generally reaching only about 3 feet.

No magnolias grow at Magnolia Point in Seattle, but madronas do now and did when early exploring settlers mistook them for the magnolias of the South, nostalgic memories not being too accurate. This *(below left)* is the blossom of one of the magnolia flourishing in southern and milder northern states.

This magnolia, *(below) Magnolia stellata* is not likely to be the one settlers were remembering, being a much smaller tree.

OKANOGAN SMITH's

apple orchard

Charles H. Odegaard, Director, Washington State Parks and Recreation Commission, announced today that Okanogan County, has been placed in the National Register of Historic Places.

Hiram F. Smith's original orchard is located at Smith Point on the sloping hills which border the east side of Lake Osoyoos, a few miles south of the Canadian border. Within the Okanogan Valley, the area is sheltered and enjoys mild winters and notably sunny and warm summers. Only six of the original apple trees survived out of 1,200 planted in 1856-57 but they still bear fruit.

Smith was born in Kennebec County, Maine, on June 11, 1829, and in the early 1850's moved to Washington territory. As a mail carrier from the Hudson's Bay Company post at Hope, British Columbia to Washington territory points, he passed through the Okanogan Valley. He resolved to build his home here and took up squatters rights.

While still engaged as a mail carrier, he obtained 1,200 small apple trees from Fort Hope, wrapped them in a small box or a blanket, and transported them, in 1856-57, by packhorse and snowshoe to his homestead. Eventually, he planted twenty-four acres of apples on the slopes along the east shore of the lake.

Smith served in the territorial and state legislatures at which time it is assumed he received the name "Okanogan" Smith. Greatly respected by all, this genial, honest, fair-minded man also earned the title of "Father of Washington State's Million Dollar Apple Industry" as well as "Father of Okanogan County". He founded an industry which spread to the benchlands and valleys of Central and Eastern Washington, covering a production area of tens of thousands of acres.

The National Register of Historic Places records the tangible reminders of the history of the United States and is the official schedule of the nation's cultural property that is worth saving. A property placed in the National Register has provided a degree of protection from arbitrary alteration and destruction by federally funded projects and the owner is eligible for consideration to receive grant-in-aid funds to assist in the restoration of the property.

The body which recommends properties to the National Register is the Washington State Advisory Council on Historic Preservation, Art Skolnik, Executive Director; Mrs. Carolyn Feasey, Chairman.

Article appeared in **Gazette-Tribune,** *Oroville, Okanogan County, Washington, December 18, 1975.*

One of old apple trees on pioneer homestead of "Okanogan Smith" is this giant specimen of early day variety, *Gloria Mundi*, an "exhibition" fruit attaining enormous size, often weighing 2 pounds or more. It is now seldom seen, replaced by apples having other qualities beyond mere size. Pictured here is orchard owner David Thorndike, now deceased, widow still residing on property. Larry L. McGraw who took photo is pomologist for Oregon Historical Society, his enthusiasm leading him to establish McGraw Experimental Gardens in Portland, Oregon, where he is propagating almost every variety of pome fruits with emphasis on historic varieties.

Okanogan Smith is credited with bringing 1,200 apple trees to his Okanogan Valley, Washington, homestead in 1850s. Exact numbers, dates and modes of transportation are uncertain but it is known some came by pack train he operated, last journey about 1861. 12 trees survive to serve as living memorials to now huge apple industry in valley.

Winesap tree pictured here is one of group of four and clearly displays characteristic pattern of sturdy limbs. The four produced 112 boxes of fruit in 1918 and still bear well. (Photo and story courtesy Mrs. David (Josephine) Thorndike.

Old photo of Okanogan Smith's original cabin still standing on property but now boarded up for protection and used as tool shed. For a time it served as first Canadian-U.S. Custom House being close to border. Here Okanogan Smith brought his 14-year old bride Mary, daughter of Indian Chief Manuel. Some time later he moved her to another cabin, then married Nancy, a white girl from Seattle. He later contracted a disease from which he died in Seattle. He was buried in historic Lake View Cemetery in grave adjoining that of famous Seattle pioneer, Henry Yesler. It is said that when his second wife appeared at old homestead to collect her inheritance, the original one attacked her with skillet, the Indian winning over the white in this battle. Mary later met death by drowning. (Photo and story courtesy Mrs. David Thorndike).

Keen signted Casey Kendall, Portland, "reads" shape, size and form of exposed root, part of gigantic Douglas fir. Trying to imagine himself sightless since
birth he will walk slowly along entire length of fallen tree to get mental picture
of tree when standing. Setting for trail is centered in lush growth of timber and
ground cover typical of forests along eastern flank of Cascade Mountains in
Oregon.

The
BRAILE TRAIL

Are the blind, the elderly, the physically handicapped to be denied the "outdoor experience"? Not in Oregon. Dedicated workers lead the way to their enjoyment of the Johnny Creek Nature Trail. Writing in January, 1974 issue of *The Lion,* Susan Saul tells of the volunteer efforts to expand the world of unfortunates in the Eugene, Oregon, area.

"Lying on the banks of rushing, tumbling Fall Creek, the site is a tangled mass of vine maple and moss covered stumps. Douglas fir and western hemlock trees tower above. Glossy leaved salal, bushy huckleberry and lush ferns disguise the rotting fallen logs that litter the forest floor. Soft carpeting of shaggy moss and fir needles blankets the earth. Rustlings in the leafy undergrowth hint of the wildlife inhabitants.

The place is steeply hilled on one side and a small, frothy stream dashes through the middle on its way to merge with Fall Creek. This spot, alternately warmed by a shifting pattern of sun flecks and nourished by the incessant rain, is typical of the lower elevation forest which covers the western slope of Oregon's Cascade Mountains like a fur coat.

It would be impossible for a person in a wheelchair or braces to penetrate this dense growth and experience the natural scene. A blind person would have extreme difficulty hiking through this tangled forest interior. How then can a handicapped person take a real walk through these woods?

Modifications can change such an outdoor area, frustrating and hazardous for the blind and physically handicapped, to one that provides persons of any age and ability a happy and memorable experience. The key is the removal of natural barriers, a key supplied in this case through a project spearheaded by the Lions of the Eugene, Oregon, area. The efforts of these Lions, with help from recreation students at the University of Oregon and the staff of the Willamette National Forest, made it possible for anyone to enjoy a leisurely walk through this forest. After a year and a half of planning, working and developing, they have transformed this site into the Johnny Creek Nature Trail for the blind and physically handicapped. A gentle, nearly level, paved half mile trail wends through the area (a second half-mile "loop" is in the planning stages), crossing back and forth on wooden bridges over swirling Johnny Creek. Interpretive signs in both braille and conventional lettering mark 19 stations which inform the hiker of the plant life and other natural beauties that surround him.

The Johnny Creek Trail uses to its best advantage the interior of the woods where the sounds of man and machine are muted and the life of the forest easier to observe. The snap of a twig, the whispering flutter of leaves, the resiny fragrance of wood, the song of a bird, the damp smell of mossy rocks along the creek banks, the gentle rustle of an unfelt wind in the tree tops and the warmth from the tree-filtered sun are amplified in the otherwise cool and quiet forest interior.

This trail is part of a recreation complex which also includes Broken Bowl Picnic Grounds, about two miles downstream from Johnny Creek. Here, facilities are adapted for the handicapped.

The idea for this pioneering development, the first of its kind in the Pacific Northwest; and one of a handful in the country designed for both the blind and the physically handicapped, originated with Richard Lilja. At that time he was the recreation officer for the Lowell Ranger District of the Willamette National Forest which administers the Fall Creek area. He realized the blind and the handicapped wanted a place where they could get out in the forest and walk. The Fall Creek area seemed a logical place for the development since its low elevation makes it accessible for year-round use and it is close to the populous (approx. 80,000 residents) Eugene area.

While the Willamette National Forest assumed responsibility for the construction of Broken Bowl, Lilja and a fellow Forest Service employee, Robert Tokarczyk of the Eugene Lions Club, brought the trail idea to the Eugene Lions early in 1971. The club volunteered to finance and build two one-half mile loop trails equipped with nylon guide ropes and braille nature signs. The supervision of planning and trail construction was handed to Roger Smith, a club member with extensive outdoor hiking experience.

The objective of both the Forest Service and the Lions club was to construct facilities to accommodate the blind and physically handicapped, yet be similar to facilities used by the sighted and non-handicapped. They had to be such that the handicapped could use them with as little assistance as possible. Their joint philosophy offered no room for over-protectiveness. The watchword was modification.

Staff from the Forest Service initiated the planning by walking over the site—1600 feet by 600 feet—and gridding the area with cords every 100 feet. They then inventoried every plant in every square, indicated items of interest, and plotted the results onto a map.

At this point, a University of Oregon class on Issues in Environmental Interpretation joined the project. As one of the class assignments, the students designed a trail through the Johnny Creek property. They went out to the site in early spring, sloshing through the mud and rain, climbing over logs and crawling under bushes to look at the indicated items of interest. Keeping in mind the design objectives, the students developed and flagged a hypothetical trail.

'Each student turned in recommendations for the trail signs for the non-sighted along with alternate signs for the sighted, but physically handicapped,' said Professor Phyllis Ford, the class instructor. 'A committee of students compiled all the papers and chose excerpts from each to reach the final recommendations which were then submitted to the Forest Service.'

Features were chosen that are easy for a blind person to examine. The students suggested sandblasting a large stump so the rings could be felt; encouraging the hikers to hug a large fir tree trunk and estimate its size; inviting the hikers to walk along the length of a 300-foot fallen tree to realize the height. Numerous stops would point out native plants close enough to be touched.

The Forest Service basically followed these recommendations and used the messages the students had written for the trail signs. But there was one major difference. The students suggested separate signs for the sighted with different messages than those for the blind, indicating less tactile experiences. Instead, the signs are clear plastic with raised braille dots, backed with written words saying the same thing.

Meanwhile, Lions Smith and Tokarczyk presented a map indicating the proposed trail and interpretive stops to a Lions board meeting and received final confirmation for the project. The board also decided to have the trail built

Trail is smoothed for easy walking by blind and physically handicapped. For most part winding trail here parallels 250' log. At right, not quite in photo, is stout wire suspended at proper height for frequent contact with tapping cane. Entire project is planned as "do it yourself" effort.

professionally. According to Smith, the practicalities of the situation showed it was not feasible to use the original idea of all volunteer labor. The club contracted to have the clearing and grading done, and a two inch asphalt tread put on the trail for $2,600. That left the Lions with building the bridges, erecting the interpretive signs, installing the posts for the guide rope and completing the remaining details.

The money for the trail paving contract came from the estate of John Mikesell, a Lion for many years and real estate man in Eugene. Mikesell left the club a tenth of his estate to be used in work for the blind.

The Lions Club of Coburg, a suburb north of Eugene, volunteered to do the parking lot. The Lions contributed the gravel, and graded and spread the circular, drive-through lot. Extra wide parking slots at the trail heads were designed to accommodate the loading and unloading of wheelchairs, crutches and walkers.

Several lumber yards and mills donated the building materials—logs, timbers, signs and guide rope posts. Smith estimates the Lions spent only six or seven dollars for materials. In contrast, the Forest Service estimates that if it were to have hired contractors to build the entire trail, it would have cost around $14,000.

It took four weekends to do the actual work on the trail. 'Guys who had never been in the outdoors before saw what we were doing, became enthusiastic and joined us,' said Lion Smith.

In addition to the Lions, three to five Forest Service personnel from the Lowell Ranger Station turned out each weekend to help with the work.

Smith was generous in his praise of their help. 'It made a difference. They furnished the know-how and the tools, so we didn't have to spend time looking up plans and instructions for bridge building.' "

111

Solitary giants like this are seldom seen, ordinarily being easy targets of lightning and wind. This specimen over 300′ tall is photographed from author's camp along Eel River, California.

The
TALLEST TREES

It seems fitting that the two largest trees in the world are growing in a state known for its superlatives and that each of the two is largest in its own way—one the bulkiest, one the tallest. For years the "tallest tree in the world" was thought to be a *Sequoia sempervirens* in the Founders Grove south of Dyerville, California. It stands 364 feet in height, is 47 feet around at the base. Current title holder is one discovered in 1963 by the National Geographic Society.

The new champion is included in a group of trees on a bend of Redwood Creek that, as of this writing, are the tallest yet found. One tree measures 367.8 feet high, with a diameter of 14 feet, and is believed to be 2,200 years old. Several trees nearby are only slightly younger and less tall. This Tall Tree Group can be reached in summer only, by a 16-mile round trip hike along a beautiful trail bordering Redwood Creek and often along its sandy bottom. For that reason, this trail is open only in summer after the rains are entirely over and the creek is down. Since there is little climbing involved, the walk is not too strenuous for experienced hikers. The trail starts near the junction of U.S. 101 and Bald Hills Road and offers the reward of taking you through a fine area of virgin redwood forest especially chosen for inclusion in the new Redwood National Park.

Within the 26 state redwood parks, three of which are included in the authorized boundaries of Redwood National Park, there are many miles of trails, including self-guiding nature trails, through magnificent groves of old-growth trees. Many of these groves were given to the state by private donors, and many other groves were purchased over the last 50 years by SAVE-THE-REDWOODS LEAGUE and given to the State.

Although observed by explorers much earlier the coastal redwood was first officially recognized and named *Taxodium distichum* by Lambert, an English botanist, the name later being changed to *Sequoia sempervirens,* then the only sequoia known. Years later, when discovered, the giant species of the Sierra experienced similar confusion. Seeds sent to England produced trees first classed as *Wellingtonia* in honor of the famous British soldier-statesman.

While the wood of the giant sequoia is extremely brittle and suitable only for fence posts and shingles, that of the coast redwood is remarkably straight grained, resilient and durable, in demand for hundreds of purposes including building lumber. This difference is caused by the autumnal part of the annular rings, much thicker in the redwood because of the more protracted growing season in the milder climate of the coast.

"It's hard to see the forest for the trees" is particularly true in photographing trees growing densely in groves. This group *(above)* in Rockefeller Grove is advantageously exposed at edge of small stream, photographed from other side. Most tree trunks are entwined with luxurious growths of poison oak. Here brilliantly colored fall foliage of nefarious vine has just fallen, leaving bare stems.

Raymond House, Portland, gives scale to "Siamese Twins" in Rockefeller Grove *(center)*. Spectacular formation may result from pair of seedlings starting life too close together, or perhaps as sprouts from long-vanished stump. Nearly perfect circles are sometimes observed where dozens of sprouts have sprung from adventitious buds always present in redwoods, stronger ones only surviving.

Some estimates give 80% of redwood trees as products of regeneration rather than seeds. This would account for dense stands as compared to more isolated specimens of giant Sierra sequoias. Sometimes such a pair as above will have completely joined trunks, forming "flatiron trees" of great dimension in one direction, narrow in other. One of these stands some feet away from this twin specimen.

Well known "Drive Through Tree" at Myer's Flat, California, *(above)* along Avenue of Giants (old Highway 101) is typical of several. Known as "Shrine Tree" it is truncated and hollow but still almost 200′ high with circumference of 64′, diameter 21′. Age is posted as 5,000 years but mature trees are usually estimated as being 500 to 1,000 years old. Even annual ring counts are apt to be misleading and difficult to assess. Eminent naturalist John Muir is now considered to have overestimated age of sequoias. "Shrine Tree" is privately owned and operation commercial but tourists driving through it often stop inside, place palms on flat sides as if trying to comprehend age.

From combined measurements of bulk, circumference, height, this "Giant Tree" *(opposite top)* is among largest *Sequoia sempervirens.* Author and schnauser Lady Flaskebo give scale to huge tree. *(Opposite bottom right).* When author photographed "Giant Tree" plaque had been stolen. Later, Henry Richards, Ranger II, Humboldt Redwoods State Park, supplied him with negatives made earlier.

Detailed foliage of *Sequoia sempervirens,* coastal redwood, *(opposite bottom left)* is less rough to touch than that of *gigantea* but still raspy. Photo made in early fall shows buds already forming for next spring's growth. This longer period of growth is contrasted with "big brother's" in Sierra foothills, 6,000 to 8,000 feet elevation, making greater toughness of wood.

When young householder Tosaldo Johnson came home to supper one night, his bride Addie, greeted him with excitement, "I found that lost lamb today. It was in the most beautiful grove we have on our land. I knew right then that if something happened to me I'd like to be buried there." And something did. She died in childbirth about two years later. Remembering her wishes young Johnson placed her body in the grove. The wooden marker rotted away but in recent years it was replaced by California Division of Beaches and Parks. Author, finding area inaccessible due to severe floods on Bull Creek Flats, is indebted to Division for this photo *(above)* expecially taken for him.

The PINES

Photo of solitary foxtail pine, *(opposite) Pinus Balfouriana*, was made on one of author's ascents of Mount Whitney in California's High Sierra. John Jeffrey, Scottish explorer and discoverer of species, disappeared while threading mountain trails alone. In his book *A Natural History of Western Trees*, Donald Culross Peattie writes, "The foxtail pine is . . . a solitary creature. Where it grows in the southern Sierra . . . on glacial cirques on land scoured by ice, it has frequently no other tree to keep it company."

Elevation here on east slope of Mount Whitney is about 11,000'. Canyon below leads down to Whitney Portals, eventually to town of Lone Pine in Owens Valley. In distance is Panamint Range, beyond that Death Valley. Area in background is home of famed bristlecone pines, oldest living things.

Bishop pines here *(above)* grow on bluffs completely exposed to wild winter winds at Mendocino, California. Instead of attaining ultimate vertical growth of 75' as in protected places they barely get up to 40' when beaten down by gales.

Many trees have at least one outstanding, simple characteristic by which definite identification in botanical keys is made easier. In the large family of pines this conspicuous quality is number of leaves or needles grouped in each bundle on the twig. Although several different species have the same number, selection becomes less broad. In the case of the most prominent, most numerous and one of the most noble pines of the west, *Pinus ponderosa*, western yellow pine, there are bundles of three leaves, 5″ to 10″ long. Cones are 3″ to 5″ long, prickles pointing outward. If one is gripped closely bare hand will quickly feel this quality.

Lewis and Clark noted these trees on their way westward, first clue being some cones floating down White River near its confluence with the Missouri in Montana. These specimens were buried in a cache at the foot of Lemhi Pass when they crossed into Idaho but when retrieved on the return journey were too rotted to be of any use. They did gather a few fresh cones on the eastward route near the present Orofino, Idaho, were brought home safely but not identified at that time.

Meriweather Lewis planned to name this and other specimens but came to an untimely death. He had referred to the cones as "burrs" and midwesterners still use that term.

"In the Bend area, there are two world champions and one runner-up that do not get the attention usually accorded suth champions. One is the largest Peachleaf Willow, one is the largest Thinleaf Alder and the runner-up is the second largest Ponderosa Pine.

"Till 1973, the Pine was the champion, but it was unseated by a California Ponderosa discovered in 1973. The California tree aced out Oregon's by only 8 points primarily because it is a little taller than the Bend area tree.

"The former champion Ponderosa Pine is located on the road which leaves U.S. 97 about 14 miles north of La Pine and goes west to the La Pine Recreation Area. There is a sign pointing north 3.3 miles west of U.S. 97 saying 'Big Tree' and the tree is located near a parking area a short distance from the road.

"This magnificent Ponderosa *(opposite)* is 162 feet high, 27 feet 11 inches in circumference with a spread of 45 feet. The trunk is 8.6 feet in diameter. There is an asphalt trail leading to the tree from the parking lot."—from The Oregon Motorist, June, 1975

Although other pines may have two, three, four or five needles to the bundle, several species sharing same characteristics, the nut pine, *Pinus monophylla*, has only one, is unique in that respect. Each needle is round in cross section. This close up photo *(below)* of sprig from author's tree on left, grown from seed collected at Rockland, Nevada, is compared with twig of ponderosa pines, three-needled, at right.

This ponderosa pine *(above)* has chosen to grow inside grave enclosure in old cemetery in Idaho City, Idaho. Comparatively recent marker near enclosure reads—"Joseph Kelley 1827-1869"

Pinus Sabiniana, Digger pine was a major food supply for Digger Indians who once occupied areas favored by the tree. The aborigines harvested nuts in large quantities, storing them for winter when wild onions and other roots were not easily located. Needles of Digger pine are in threes, long, grayish and flexible, giving tree wilted, unhealthy look, casting almost no shade for travelers.

Typical specimens of nut pines *(above center)* are shown here flanking old hotel at Rockland, Nevada. Growth of these trees is slow due to harsh climate in foothills of Great Basin where most are found, plus lack of water and soil nutrients.

Areas preferred by Digger pines *(above right)* are all around mountainous edges of Great Central Valley of California, this typical one being at extreme northern fringe, near Shasta Dam. It shows characteristic branching pattern assumed by trunk.

Cone of nut or pinon pine requires two years to attain maturity. First year cones are bright chartreuse and liberally bedecked with drops of resinous pitch which is extremely fragrant. Christmas wreath made for friend still smelled good after several seasons of display.

Clearly seen in photo are nuts so prized by Indian tribes that many white men have been killed for cutting down the trees. These seeds remained intact for photo on long trip from Rockland, Nevada, to Portland, Oregon, only by tenderly cradling cone in softly padded box.

Author can only guess why one pine, *Pinus monophylla*, (one-needled pine) is called nut pine, while another, *Pinus edulis*, with two needles to the bundle and also valued for its nuts is commonly called pinon pine. Probably it is because the latter, growing in areas such as Arizona where Spanish language is often used (pino is Spanish for pine). Nut pine, found mostly in and around Nevada, is not so subject to Spanish influence. The pinon pine shown here grows beside mule trail at Grand Canyon, Arizona. Tree of this size can easily bee 100 years old.

Pinon pine clings tenaciously to precarious perch on canyon side in Zion National Park. Strange formations, left and right, are in effect petrified sand dunes, area sometimes termed "Fossil Sahara". Sand formations were under the sea for ages, then deposits of limestone and shale were added. Eventually lifted to surface, layers were eroded by river and natural sandblasting, once again exposed to view.

This is pinon pine growing exposed to vicious winds and long seasons without sufficient moisture near Panguitch, Utah, not far from Cedar Breaks.

Whitebark pines, *Pinus*, growing in chosen habitat, at upper limits of mountain tree growth, termed "Timberline". This specimen *(above)* grows at about 7,000' on southeast slope of Mount Hood. White River Glacier, center, is shown almost in its entirety, typical of glaciers in general. It is now much shrunken, having at least once in former times filled entire canyon. Conceivably, with climatic changes, it should do so again.

The sugar pine, *(above center) Pinus Lambertiana*, is in many ways the most noble of the family, often towering to height of 200', ranking after sequoias and Douglas firs, taking fourth place in American trees. At least one specimen in California's Stanislaus National Forest is 32' in circumference at 4½' from ground. Cones are the largest or at least longest, sometimes reaching nearly 2'. Lower limbs (about 100' from ground) can be 40' long. Note cones at lower right. Sugar pines shown grow in Calaveras Grove with giant sequoias as close neighbors.

Norfolk Island pines are known as a favorite pot plant, branching horizontally in symmetrical, star-shaped patterns. Natives of temperate Norfolk Islands, these trees grow to mature size in frost-free areas such as here in Coronado, California.

Skeleton of old pinon pine stands on brink of Arizona's Grand Canyon.

Heavy frost outlines needles of whitebark pine. They are bunched more than usual, tree being grown by author as bonzai specimen.

Pines grow sparsely in nearly sterile granite around tiny lake in glacial cirque near divide between Mount Whitney and Mount Langley in High Sierra, California. Although not positively identifiable now, prominent tree at left is almost surely foxtail pine, *Pinus Balfouriana*, because of location and general appearance. Altitude here is about 11,000', the approximate timberline.

Pinon pines growing in narrow zone in Bryce Canyon, Utah, *(above)* where eroded material is loose enough to soak up and retain some moisture. Sculptured cliffs assume many imagined forms, often bearing such names as Queen Victoria. Color is brilliant salmon pink.

Stand of Bishop pine, *(above center) Pinus muricata*, pictured against foggy background near Mendocino, California. This pine is something of a curiosity among botanists in that it has so many varieties in such a restricted range. A few are found near San Vicente, Baja California, with scattered groves northward along coast of central and northern California. Small group on Santa Cruz Island was at first named *Pinus remorata* (1930), then regrouped with other muricatas. Some botanists suggest that species be divided into four. All have two leaves to the bundle, very thick bark up to 6″.

First of this species to be identified and named by botanist Thomas Coulter was found near San Luis Obispo, accounting for common name, Bishop pine. Cones are reluctant to fall, often hanging on for many years, to point of often becoming ensnared in growing limbs and bark, even buried completely, seeds and all. In this photo note cone clusters on upper branches. These specimens grow well back from ocean, partly protected from fiercest winds. Contrast their upright growth with other pines pictured in this section.

Whitebark pine *(above), Pinus albicaulis*, grows at timberline on all Cascade peaks, this one on south slope of Mount Hood at about 7,000'. This alpine species rarely attains maximum of 60', usually about 6' to 20'. Leaves are in bundles of five, about 2" long, cones also about 2" long. Photo was made in November on morning after new snowfall, total depth here about 5'.

Cones of Digger pine are enormous, up to a foot long, weighing several pounds when green. Hanging on tree persistently for long periods, they are conspicuous along roads to Highway 49 that threads gold camps. Author brought this one home from near Coloma to photograph it under controllable lights. Note seeds or pine nuts, about ¾″ long.

The WILLOWS

Famed, romantic Rio Grande River flows slowly here, respectfully approaching spectacular Santa Elena Canyon with its vertical walls up to 1,800' high. For much of its length as it does here river forms boundary between U.S. and Mexico. Dense stands of brushy willows screen banks making excellent cover for Mexicans attempting to enter this country illegally. Here they can hide until coast is clear, dash across to hide again. Sometimes there are prearranged meetings with friends already established on this side. In this wild, unpopulated Big Bend area such entries are comparatively easy until Mexican reaches nearest town, at this point, Presidio, Texas. Both banks offer richest variety of cacti species to be found anywhere.

Weeping willow is loathe to lose its leaves in fall. Here in Portland, Oregon's Westmoreland Park, we have complete denudation, aptly showing beautiful structure of limb and twig. Absolute nudity is of short duration. Early in spring mist of chartreuse surrounds tree, tender color remaining even after full leafage has taken place. Later in summer foliage darkens.

Great Swedish botanist, Linnaeus, responsible for tremendous task of giving plants world-wide classification, was under misapprehension when he considered weeping willow. He thought it came from Babylonian regions and christened it *Salix babylonica*. Actually China was its ancestral home. Tree attains great size, bark on larger specimens roughly corrugated, bole often contorted in picturesque manner. This one grows in Portland, Oregon's Westmoreland Park near lawn bowling green.

Eloquent message of sad farewell is shown in conventionalized weeping willow, clasped hands. This monument is in Buena Vista, Oregon.

This weeping willow was photographed on heavily overcast winter day just before head gardener at Portland Memorial Mausoleum began monumental task of individually pruning each slender branch. Ends of boughs will appear as stubby "heads" or "polls", giving rise to term for drastic pruning - to "pollard". With willows this operation is never ceasing, new growth so vigorous as to defeat purpose. Examples of pollard trees of slower growing nature, are frequently seen in painting of French scenes and roadsides.

Champion peach leaf willow shows braided bark texture seldom attained in willows of more moderate size.

Weeping willow in stylized form has long been favored as decoration on tombstones. This one in Catholic Cemetery in Mendocino, California, is inscribed: "Wm. Fainter, Sheriff of Mendocino County. He was drowned Oct 30, 1863. Aged 31 yrs, 5 mo. Sleep on, Billy. Take thy rest. Our God hath done what He thought best."

Some trees do not seem to be particularly huge yet are rated as best in their field. A case in point is this world champion peach leaf willow, *Salix amygdaloides*. This unique tree grows in a park setting at Bend, Oregon, on banks of Deschutes River. Stream here gives no clue as to its turbulent character along most of its course which makes it deserving of its French name meaning "river of the falls."

Although the peach leaf willow is described in botany keys as reaching height of 60' to 70', this specimen stands 83' with spread of 70' and girth of 13' taken 4½' above ground. Willows generally provide problems in determining trees from shrubs. Some bushy ones rise the 8' in stature considered necessary to be tree. Others more tree-like, degenerate to shrubs in localities lack-

ing in moisture or nutrients. The peach willow, given a well watered location, as near a stream, is almost always a true tree.

San Luis Rey was largest, most populous of California Missions. Most of complex is open to visitors but this area, called "The Padre's Garden", is reserved for privacy. The author was graciously permitted to make these photographs. This is general view *(opposite)* of garden which shelters oldest pepper tree in California *(right)*. Foliage detail is seen in branch of younger tree at extreme left. Near center is flowering stalk of agave, often called century plant. Actually, plant blooms when mature, around 25 years of age, then dies. Several young specimens already growing around base will replace original.

California's oldest PEPPER TREE

The California pepper tree, *Schinus molle*, bears pendulous clusters of small, coral red berries. Each berry is centered by single black seed that resembles "peppercorns" of true pepper, *Piper nigrum*, no relation at all. However, pungent seeds were ground and used as condiment by mission fathers in early days when seasonings were scarce.

This highly ornamental tree was more extensively planted than any other excepting the eucalyptus in early days of state. Not only is foliage softly green, swaying in slightest breeze, but it can stand long periods of drought, subsisting only on short season of scant rainfall. Its popularity has waned in recent years because of its susceptibility to black scale, a disease easily transmitted to citrus fruits grown in same area. Many thousands of handsome old specimens have been destroyed because of their proximity to citrus groves.

Native of Peru, story of its introduction to California has similarities to that of apple tree brought to Pacific Northwest. It is related that, in 1830, when group of sailors walking along road from residential district of Lima, Peru, to their ship waiting in harbor, came to a pepper tree, one man ripped off a handful of attractive rose colored berries and dropped them in his pocket. Their voyage brought them to Oceanside, California where crew were dinner guests of San Luis Rey Mission padres. Conversation included local climate, so similar to sailors' homeland, trees and plants that could be grown in this new land. So pepper seeds were produced and presented to hosts.

Tremendous gnarled bole shows great age of California's original pepper tree. It is sole survivor of group planted in 1830.

The FIRS • HEMLOCKS • SPRUCES

Narrow, pencil thin Alpine firs thrive in Blue Mountains of Oregon, these at old mining camp of Greenhorn. Ponderosa pines and other firs are inter-mingled in stands of Alpine fir. It is related that the first miners digging in this, as yet unnamed, area were approached by stranger who asked, "Where should I dig for gold?" Pointing out an unlikely site at random, the men ig-nored him. Of course the greenhorn uncovered a lot of gold and the camp had a name.

Scene *(above)* near now ghostly mining camp of Ophir in Colorado's Rockies is idyllic in June when this photo was made. Ground is covered with golden dandelions, aspen saplings are just putting out their tender leaves and much snow remains on Ophir Needles, over 12,000' high. Growing in dark copses in middle distance are spires of Alpine firs, *Abies lasiocarpa*. These are among true firs as differentiated from those popularly termed Douglas firs. The alpine type grows at high altitudes in western mountains, thriving around 9,500' in Rocky Mountains as those shown here.

Mountain hemlocks, *(above center) Tsuga Mertensia*, after snowstorm on south slope of Mount Hood, Oregon. Technical terminology varies from Latin, Greek to Japanese, as in this case. Some species of hemlock are native to Japan, generic name, *Tsuga*, now applying to all in that family. They are almost all of two species in the western United States - mountain and coastal. Former type is usually recognized as having larger cones, up to 3" in length, those of coastal forests up to about 1'.

Unidentified tree *(above)* (very likely Coast
hemlock) in Olympic Rain Forest which
sprouted on top of constantly moist log, growing
in this position until hanging roots penetrated
soil, thereafter straddling its host, (Photo from
Bert Kellog, Port Angeles, Wash.).

Large spruce tree grows inside grave enclosure in old Barkerville, British Columbia, cemetery. Faded copy of Barkerville *Sentinel* states that Griffith Lewis died in Royal Cariboo Hospital of "inflamation of the bowels". Barkerville is historic gold camp in northern British Columbia recently restored to semblance of its former state by provincial government.

Huge, uniquely branched Douglas fir, *(opposite) Pseudotsuga Douglasi*, stands in old cemetery at Claquato, Washington. In early 1850s Lewis Hawkins Davis and family arrived in Portland, Oregon, having crossed the plains in his covered wagon. A short stay in Willamette Valley convinced Davis that the area was already over populated. There were neighbors, he said, crowding up to half a mile from him! So the Davis family and a few other like-minded settlers crossed the Columbia River and headed north to the Chehalis River. There Davis found the Indians unfriendly but some did show him this big fir on the hill and said he could make a temporary camp under its sheltering branches. The stay became a permanent one, town of Claquato growing up near tree. Now plaque on trunk identifies giant fir as "The Pioneer Tree".

Noble stand of Western red cedar. Not a true cedar and although technically termed *Thuja plicata*, it is so generally known as red cedar it is so designated here. Range of this magnificent tree in the west is very wide - from Portage Bay in maritime Alaska to California's fog belt native to Coast redwood and eastward to Bitterroot Mountains in Idaho and Montana. Those growing near Orofina, Idaho, furnished canoe logs used by Lewis and Clark in their journey to Columbia River and Pacific Ocean. It is said that stumps of these were still in existence as late as 1900. Would that at least one of these had been preserved! Photo shows part of grove sheltering grave of historian Bernard De Voto, located on Lolo Pass, route actually traversed by the two famed captains in 1805.

The CEDARS

Famous "Gumdrop Trees" in Ferndale, California, are certainly the cypress, probably Lawson's *Chamaecyperus Lawsoniana*, exact identification being difficult. Mrs. Gertrude Clausen, daughter of Arnold Berding who built house on this property 101 years ago, and since deceased, related, "We have a picture of this house when it was new. Those trees were here then, were about 17 years old." Horticulturist Manning of Ferndale, recently stated, "the trees were sheared every five or six years until a few years ago. They flourished under this treatment. Then the old gentleman who had done the job for so many years passed away. About that time we began having our annual celebration in August and the new gardener sheared the trees every year just before the crowds arrived. This seems to be proving too rigorous, the trees not growing enough between times. The one at the right of the gate shows some dead areas."

Grove of incense cedars, *Libocedrus decurrensa*, grows in Hoyt Arboretum in Portland. Slender spires are indication of youth, older specimens more spreading, rather closely resembling *Sequoia gigantea*, even to heavily furrowed, reddish brown bark. Leaves are quite shiny when struck by side light. Wood is used for pencils and fence posts. Range is southern Oregon, much of California with sprinkling in Washoe County, Nevada.

Sheltering branches *(above center)* swoop low to cradle grave of famous plant wizard Luther Burbank. Locally termed Cedar of Lebanon, *Cedrus libani*, tree grows beside Burbank's home of many years in Santa Rosa, California. Lover of trees, Burbank moved here in 1875 because of great diversity of trees in this area. It is presumed he planted this cedar about 1880 and later requested that he be buried beneath it with no tombstone.

Photo *(above right)* made by Darius Kinsey in 1906 shows loggers at start of falling red cedar. At that time this goliath was considered to be largest tree in State of Washington—76′ in circumference 1½′ from ground. Today cutting down of such a tree would be considered veritable sacrilege (Photo and story from *This Was Logging* by Ralph W. Andrews).

Cones and foliage of *Cedrus atantica*. Characteristic cones, their slightly depressed apexes giving clue to species, presented problem for close up photograph, being far out of camera reach. Problem was resolved with aid of tall ladder, branch lassoed and held down within reach of lens.

Matching pair of Lawson Cypress (Port Orford cedar) *Chamaecyparis Lawsoniana*, was planted in front of Portland's venerable City Hall *(above)* just before turn of century. One fell victim to Columbus Day storm of 1962.

Park people were of opinion that tree was doomed, should be cut up and removed. William "Bill" Robinson, head gardener of Portland City Parks, held out for trying to save fine specimen. He maintained that since tree had fallen atop huge petroglyph a few feet north root system had been spared sufficiently to preserve life if tree were pulled back into place and secured with guy wires. This was done and soon

tree was again standing erect, roots carefully replaced and covered with good soil. Today it thrives as before in front of City Hall (Photo from Kodachrome by William C. Robinson, Portland).

Restored Port Orford cedar left in photo *(below)* now matches its mate, right. Petroglyph stone which prevented tree from total collapse is partially visible about 25 feet north. Two trees in center are "sweet gums" just approaching best fall coloration.

TREATY TREE *at Medicine Creek*

"The first treaty between Washington Territorial Governor Stevens and the Indians was at Medicine Creek," write Albert and Jane Salisbury in their book *Here Rolled the Covered Wagons.* "Stevens who was also Superintendent of Indian Affairs, negotiated a series of treaties, mostly unsuccessful, with the Indians during the years 1854 and 1855. Some of the tribes did not sign them. Of those who did sign, many were unsure of what they were signing despite the presence of interpreters.

"At Medicine Creek December 24 to 26, 1854, the Nisquallies, the Puyallups, the Squaxons and others contracted a treaty with Stevens in which they relinquished title to all their lands, except certain areas which were to become reservations. In general, they agreed to keep peaceful and to free all their slaves. The Indians retained their fishing and hunting rights.

"The government in return was to pay $32,500 for the land plus $3,250 to be spent on preparing and equipping the reservations. In addition the United States would set up agricultural and industrial schools, supplying the teachers.

"Edmond Meany's *History of the State of Washington* says, 'It is altogether probable that the treaties contributed to the causes of the wars that followed them.' The treaties certainly tended to show the Indians that they were to lose their homes and to be forced to accept a foreign way of life."

Council fire smoke? Prevailing haze of Nisqually Flats spreading out into Puget Sound, Washington, seems to come from old Indian campfires. (Photo by Albert Salisbury, 1948).

Close up photo of flowers of *Liriodendron tulip-fera* explains origin of both technical name and common term "tulip tree". Blossoms are similar to those of some magnolias and indeed do belong to same family, but there the similarity ends. Magnolias generally bloom in early spring and are most often white in color. The tulip tree puts forth its clusters of bloom in midsummer and they are bright orange . . . yet they cannot be fully appreciated because the heavy maple-like foliage obscures them. At close range they are most beautiful.

The tree is native to most eastern states. George Washington dug several saplings on February 8, 1785, and planted them at his home, "Mount Vernon", in Virginia. Since the trees most likely sprouted in 1776 they became known as the "Independence Tree" and in the Bicentennial Year of 1976, the Mount Vernon Ladies Association of the Union disseminated seeds from one surviving tree. Several were sent to the author to germinate. Flowers shown here are from a large tree near his home in Portland, Oregon.

COTTONWOODS • POPLARS
ASPENS

Succumbing to old age this truncated log slowly decays in Rough and Ready, California. Commonly known as black cottonwood, *Populus trichocarpa*, this member of tribe, distributed along California's Sierran gold belt up to an elevation of 10,000', is easily the largest.

Rough and Ready was roaring gold camp in 1850's. That population had strong feeling of independence is shown by fact town once "seceded" from Union as protest against any form of restricting laws intended to keep the peace. During this period, according to local legend, a beautiful slave girl arrived in town having been bought by local miner. She liked to ride and would often break off a switch from a handy tree to speed up her mount. Once she dismounted and thrust the switch into the ground. It took root and sprouted readily as cottonwoods do. Tree lived on long after town went ghost and only recently had to be cut down as hazard to few people still there. Old building in background was village blacksmith shop.

Giant cottonwood *(above)* shelters graves of Chipeta and her husband, the great Chief Ouray, in cemetery on Ute Reservation at Ignacio, Colorado. For many years Chief Ouray maintained shaky peace between his people and whites. In 1850 he chose a beautiful Tabeguache girl for his wife. The greatest tragedy of couple's life was untimely death of their son who was abducted by Kiowas. Before his death in 1881, embittered by long friction with whites, Ouray asked his people never to reveal his burial place. When Chipeta died, however, his remains were exhumed and buried at her side.

Graceful cottonwoods *(above center)* gather naturally in small groves near Maryhill, Washington. This level area along northern bank of Columbia River was site of Washington terminus of ferries operating from Oregon for many years. Modern bridge a mile west now replaces them. Picnic park maintained by State of Washington lies among trees, sites for tables selected for protection from strong winds almost continuously blowing up or down Columbia gorge.

New Era, Oregon, is a tiny community along
the Willamette River just above historic Oregon
City. Villagers at one town believed town was
destined for a great future and named it accordingly. The general area had a sufficiently
large Catholic population to justify building a
church around the turn of the century. Priest
who must have loved trees planted small Lombardy poplars, one at each side of steps to building. Some years later church burned to the
ground but young trees were spared and pair
stand today, *(above right)* marking nearby old
cemetery from afar.

One of the most striking and widely distributed trees is the Lombardy poplar, *(below) Populus nigra*, variety *italica*. It originated from a single cutting, a sport on a conventional type *nigra* on the plains of Lombardy about 1710. This tree is seen everywhere in the country and is especially popular as a wind break in arid, windy sections of the western states. Group in photo grows low on eastern slope of the Sierra along road leading to Mammoth Lakes. The tree has a strong tendency to sucker out at the base, at once contributing to its easy propagation and its propensity to rob neighboring areas of moisture and sustenance. For this reason it is eminently suitable to large, unguarded areas. It becomes a pest where control is desirable. This trait is very noticable in photo.

Near now ghostly mining camp of Ophir in Colorado's Rocky Mountains is this old cemetery *(below center)*. Aspens growing at this altitude, 9,400′, are tiny, having only short season to grow between snows. Although photo was made in June, leaves are just emerging. Color is tender green, exactly right to complement dazzling gold of countless dandelion blossoms covering ground.

Satiny trunks of "Quaking Aspen", *(below)* *Populus tremuloides*, are near white with faintest touch of light green. Scars where old limbs have fallen in self-pruning process form "eyes", marking aspen for easy recognition. Leaves have flattened surface that acts as pivot so least movement of air sets them quaking or trembling. Early missionaries in West related how mountain men had superstition that these trees furnished wood for The Cross, therefore trembling ever since. In autumn leaves turn yellow, most brilliant hue of any tree, causing what seems to be golden rivers flowing down high slopes.

Trunks of black cottonwoods at Maryhill, Washington, show characteristic
smooth, light colored upper parts contrasting with roughly dark furrowed
boles. This somber grove grows along edge of shallow "draw" often filled with
water during and after heavy rains. Cottonwoods are often called "balsams"
because their sticky springtime buds exude a sweet fragrance noticeable for
long distances. Although lacking definite flat leaf stems that cause leaves of
their relatives, the aspens, to "quake", yet cottonwoods do flutter in strong
breezes in this area, alternately showing darker upper sides and silvery
reverse. Both members of *Populus*, cottonwoods and aspens are in some areas
heavily logged for pulpwood, although the short fibered product must be mixed with spruce or other long fibered pulp. In late spring when seed pods, strung
along the old catkin ripen, they burst forth with a white, cotton-like downy
sail to fill the air, giving rise to the popular name. These trees are also depicted
in the end sheets of this book.

Southeastern section of Oregon is sparsely settled, roads and towns few and far between. Some areas have been only temporarily populated by sheep herders for years. In one of these lonely sectors, southeast of tiny French Glen, is grassy flat near Fish Lake, called Naughty Girl Meadows. In '20s and early' 30s, during months of highest sheep concentration, one "madam" in Portland found it profitable to make long journey with a bevy of her girls and set up tent city in meadows.

The sheep herders cooperated gratefully and formed their own flocks. Those in waiting line would pass away time by inscribing messages and appropriate drawings on the smooth white aspen trunks, sometimes listing prices madam charged for their welfare. Most inscriptions are not in good taste here but William Crispin of Portland, skilled camera repairman and avid photographer of wild life, recently made some records of them. One is this "aspenglyph" depecting what seems to be fancy coffee pot.

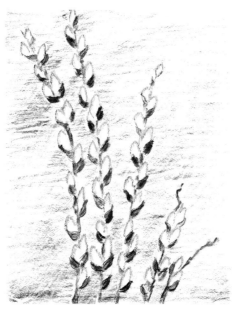

Champion thinleaf alder. Pacific Coast residents are familiar with Oregon or red alder, whitish or grey of trunk, showing red underneath when wounded. The thinleaf alder, *Alnus sinuata*, is so different as to have escaped detection for some time during author's search for it.

Described in tree guides as "Thinleaf or Sitka alder, a slender shrub or small tree, ranging from coast of Alaska to one mile southeast of Crescent City, California, 5 to 40 feet high."

This champion is largest of any known individual measuring 4 feet 9 inches in circumference (standard girth measurements are taken at 4½ feet above ground), 42 feet high with spread of 36 feet. Genial Douglas Cook, 90 years of age, stands proudly here beside his very own "world's champion" at 1710 Steidel St. Bend, Oregon. Deschutes River is shown grossly overexposed in sunny background.

FOURTH *of* JULY TREE

Carving on white pine marks historic spot on Mullan Road now named "Fourth of July Canyon" in Idaho.

Albert and Jane Salisbury wrote of landmarks and highlights along pioneer trails west in their book *Here Rolled the Covered Wagons*, in which photo appears. One historic trail was the Mullan Road through Idaho. "Hacking out 624 miles of road in the 19th century was a tremendous and perilous undertaking. The Mullan Road, built for military purposes, was one of the most noted of the early wagon trails.

"It extended from Fort Benton, where navigation on the Missouri River ceased, to Walla Walla. About 100 men under Lt. John Mullan started construction at Walla Walla in 1858.

"Indians interfered but the men resumed work on the project in 1859. Until 1863 they labored over prairie lands, through almost impentrable forests, over the rugged Bitterroot Mountains, and across the open-timbered table lands. It was not much of a road; Father Cataldo remarked that '. . . Mullan just made enough of a trail so he could get back.'

"But those early roads were formed more by the trample of many feet and the roll of many wagons than they were by construction crews. The Mullan Road at once felt the trample and the roll, for it was a path to the gold fields as well as to the Oregon country.

"On July 4, 1861, Mullan and his road builders camped in a canyon near the present Coeur d'Alene. One of the men carved the date and his initials on a white pine tree and the gorge now bears the name Fourth of July Canyon".

The DOGWOODS

"The woods are full of 'em" but you would never know it until near end of April when suddenly clouds of white appear among sombre dark green firs of northwestern hills and valleys. A single spray as shown here has lacy effect but overall pattern on tree provides solid snowy display. Actual flowers are minute, clustered on central "nubbin". Later they are replaced by bright red drupes. About same time in fall tree will be again swathed in white when second blooming takes place. Actual flower size is about 4".

The "Pacific" dogwood is native to Northwest and Northern California areas where coastal fogs prevail. Actual flowers are very tiny, individual ones almost invisible, but grouped in clusters surrounded by circle of conspicuous white bracts. Flowers later develop into clusters of bright red berries. Autumn will often see second blooming only slightly less showy than first.

This dogwood, *Cornus nuttalli*, was pride and joy of city of Milwaukie, Oregon, few miles south of Portland. It was considered by many to be largest specimen in world, having reached height of 65′ with girth of 7′, but encyclopedias state that species may reach 80′ in height. This majestic specimen gave Milwaukie title of "Dogwood City" and one is pictured on city stationery.

The infamous Columbus Day Storm in 1962 split the venerable tree from top to bottom. Later ice storms broke down remaining branches, in a few years reducing the tree to a wreck, when it was cut down. It stood on the property of Henry Niedermeyer where now only the stump remains, left standing in the pathetic hope that a green sprout may yet appear from it. But dogwoods withstand very little damage and this one suffered more than it could endure.(Photo by Allen J. deLay, Milwaukie, Oregon).

MAPLE TREES *of* TOLLGATE

Western tollgate on Barlow Road, Oregon—scene photographed about 1895. A. J. Prideaux told author in 1970, "I joined Y.M.C.A. as a young boy. I am nearly 90 years old now but well remember those journeys to Mt. Hood on the old Barlow Road. On this trip we stopped at Tollgate for a picture. That little building was one of the few not built of rough logs."

Note young big leaf maples just back of fence, planted by Daniel Perker, early tollgate keeper. Arleigh Mitchell, keeper 1905-08, relates there was narrower passage beside main gate shown here for those on foot and small animals such as sheep. As they passed through they were counted. At 100 pebble was dropped in box nailed to post to simplify count. Cost of passage for sheep, goats, hogs was 3 cents each. (Photo Oregon Historical Society).

1975 photo made in autumn. Maples planted long ago are in brilliant yellow dress. Scene approximates that shown in 1895 photo. Metallic reproduction of that photo, made in hope of permanence, is shown here mounted on rock in front of sign. Clearly shown is vandalism done by deliberate pounding with sharp lava rock.

Close up shows gate, duplicated from old photo, and one of mossy old maples. At left in full autumn dress of brilliant red is young vine maple, *Acer circinatum* (note gracefully curving stem, giving promise of later vine-like growth).

The OAKS

Does this gigantic California black oak *(opposite)* shelter the second "Six Bit House" in tiny town of Wolf Creek, Oregon? Author was unable to settle controversy about this on his visit there to photograph tree. Several old timers, one the town's historian, gave conflicting stories. One account placed name as local term for historic, two-story tavern built in 1857, still standing, about to be restored. It was explained - when a traveler, arriving late and wishing to stay overnight, would find several kerosene lamps on fireplace mantel with instructions to place six bits there, light a lamp and go upstairs to bed. A "bit", of course referred to the Spanish real, two being equal in value to 25 cents in American money.

Lewis A. McArthur, in his *Oregon Place Names*, seems to confirm the belief that this very old log building, in exactly the situation described, is the second "Six Bit House". The item reads:

"WOLFCREEK, Josephine County. Wolfcreek is the post office for Wolf Creek community and railroad station. The place is generally referred to as two words. There were plenty of wolves in Oregon in early days, and a number of streams are known as Wolf Creek.

"Wolf Creek community was the locality of the famous Six Bit House, frequently mentioned in pioneer history. In 1936 James T. Chinnock of Grants Pass wrote the compiler about this establishment, transmitting information from James Tuffs and George Riddle of Grants Pass, both familiar with the history of southern Oregon. The original Six Bit House was built during the Indian wars, probably about 1853, within the sharp hairpin curve of the Southern Pacific Company railroad about a mile east of town. It was at the mouth of a gulch on the old road location north of the present Pacific Highway. There are several stories about the origin of the name. The most probable explanation is that 75 cents was charged for a night's lodging, compared with a dollar charged elsewhere along the road. Another story is that the proprietor interrupted some white men who were hanging an Indian nearby and declined to let them proceed with the business until the melancholy brave paid the inn-keeper six bits, then past due. This story seems fanciful to the compiler because of the improbability that a local Indian ever had six bits in currency. The building has long since disappeared, but Mr. Tuffs recalled seeing the remains during his youth.

The second Six Bit House, built of logs, was in the north part of the town, close to the railroad. Mr. Tuffs lived in it several years. The present Wolf Creek Tavern was built later and had no connection with either of the Six Bit houses."

The late Dean Collins, long time garden editor of Portland *Journal*, was well-beloved character to his readers. On one occasion he commissioned author to make series of photographs of Portland trees in winter dress (or undress?). Among those used for his story was this fine specimen of Oregon oak, *Quercus garryana*. It shows quite well the sturdy branching structure of this magnificent native of Oregon's Willamette Valley.

Gnarled, moss-dappled limbs of Oregon oak, *Quercus garryana (above)*, spread over site of gruesome murder-suicide perpetrated during heyday of Buena Vista, Oregon, once booming river port, long since ghost town. While pregnant, a Mrs. Tubbs deserted her brutal husband and fled to house beside this tree. Tubbs, having nursed his grievances at old Bust Head saloon, reeled out and around until he located his renegade wife.

While town's populace was celebrating Independence Day several reports distinctly different sounding from firecrackers were heard coming from house. Neighbors saw Mrs. Tubbs stagger out and die from bullet wounds. Her husband was found inside writhing in death from self-inflicted wounds, his old style five-shooter empty beside him. Mrs. Tubbs was buried in cemetery, her mate's body relegated to an obscure weed patch. It was soon removed by a "resurrection man" and sold to a Polk County doctor, according to legend. (Photo from *Ghost Town Treasures* by Lambert Florin).

Jack London lived out his last days here in the Valley of the Moon, half mile from Glen Ellen, California. He died at an early age from stress and strain of high living. At his farm and horse ranch he put into practice many theories of how it should be run that proved successful in all respects except financial.

Although constantly harassed by creditors and leeching friends he began each day with a furious gallop along this trail cleared through groves of "scrub oaks" and California buckeyes, native form of horse chestnuts. At more tranquil times, Jack and Charmaine would ride trail together and on one occasion he pointed out large stone, telling her, "When I die I want you to place my ashes under this stone." Natural tombstone lies a few feet from area in photo *(above center)*.

300 year old California white oak, *(above) Quercus lobata*, 18'8" in circumference at 4½' above ground, limb spread 118' shelters restored adobe home of William B. Ide, one of party of settlers that raised first Bear Flag in plaza of Sonoma, California, in effort to wrest country from Mexican control. Some limbs of tree have become very brittle. In spite of authorities' efforts to preserve and secure heavy branches with guy wires, one large one fell to ground in 1972, narrowly missing several visitors, including historians, Mr. and Mrs. Oscar Olson, now of nearby Red Bluff.

EWING YOUNG
WHO DIED IN 1841 LIES BURIED BENEATH
THIS TREE WHICH WAS PLANTED BY
MIANDA BAYLEY & SIDNEY SMITH
ON MAY 6, 1846
THIS MARKER PLACED BY
CHAMPOEG CHAPTER
DAUGHTERS OF THE AMERICAN REVOLUTION
JUNE 14, 1939

This nearly perfect specimen of Oregon oak *(opposite top)* stands near Newberg not far from Champoeg, site of Oregon's famous "Decide Meeting" (Would Oregon remain part of Great Britain or would it "secede" to United States?). Ewing Young, whose death precipitated historic "Wolf Meetings" which culminated in "Decide", lies buried under this tree. Rounded outline, shown here as nearly smooth, is even more spectacular in winter when extended twigs seem to have been contoured by hedge clippers. Level, fertile fields such as this one on French Prairie were goal of almost continuous trains of covered wagons.

Ewing Young's grave was unmarked *(opposite bottom)* until one of his farm hands, Sidney Smith, did something about it. Walking with his fiancee, Mianda Bayley, around farm, he saw grave and to commemorate Young's last resting place, planted acorn at spot.

Large Arizona live oak *(above)* stands near old store at Mowry where one of the state's oldest mines is located. During Civil War, owner, Lt. Sylvester Mowry, was accused of making lead bullets and selling them to Confederacy. Stationed at Fort Crittenden, he was interned at Yuma Penitentiary for alleged crime. Although later released, he was ruined physically and financially. Mine and town, near Mexican border, were constantly harassed by Indians. On one occasion they captured two whites, J. B. Mills and Edwin Stevens, hung them feet first from a live oak near this one and built a slow fire beneath them. Fellow miners buried them in Mowry Cemetery. Of 17 men buried there 15 had died similar violent deaths. On a recent visit to Mowry author found the buildings greatly deteriorated, even trees suffering from long periods of drought.

"Bird of Paradise Tree", *Strelitzia nicolai*, grows in semi-tropical luxuriance on grounds of Hotel Del Coronado, Coronado, California. Flowers of this tree-type are of same bird-like form but less brilliant than orange and blue "birds of paradise" sported by much better known shrubby *S. regina*.

Legend of the **MEDICINE TREE**

Ram's horn in Montana pine tree led to Indian legend and marked trail of Lewis and Clark. One of the many colorful tales of the pioneer West making up their book *Here Rolled the Covered Wagons* is the one Albert and Jane Salisbury tell of the Medicine Pine in the Bitterroot Valley and Indian lore concerning it. Photo was made in 1948 by the Salisburys.

"Ceremonial dances and tribal rituals of Salish Indians," they recount, "were performed under this medicine tree for generations. Here, on their annual pilgrimage to the Bitterroot Valley, the tribesmen made their invocations and hung offerings to the Great Spirit.

"A ram's horn was stuck into the tree in early days. On the mountainside back of the tree are several rocks resembling the profiles of Indian faces. From these facts the legend of the tree was concocted.

"There was a ram, a mountain sheep, who killed all who passed on the trail between the Bitterroot Valley and Rosses Hole. A coyote, clever as all his kind, taunted the ram about his strength. To show his power the ram charged the tree, impaling a horn in the trunk. The wily coyote killed him with a knife. Cutting off the ram's head, he threw it against the mountainside. Blood splashed about, coloring the rocks and leaving smears which looked like faces."

HANGING TREES

Unusually large ironwood tree has grisly past. 19 men died violent deaths suspended from nearly horizontal branch (left). Locale is now ghostly Vulture City near Wickenburg, Arizona. (See history in Giant Cactis section). The ironwood, *Olneya tesota*, is a rarity in several respects, one in that there is only one species. Building in background was jail. Walls were nearly impregnable and stout ceiling delayed access to frail roof. Seen nailed to tree are remains of wooden sighboard that gave some history of tree.

Hanging tree *(above)* at Kerby, Oregon, is an oak, probably California black oak. Kerby is not far from Siskiyou Mountains where this species flourishes. It is said that any old town having no hanging tree has no trees at all. Tales of several have some verifying factors such as being visible from jail or in the case of this one, being close to courthouse, actually a part of Masonic Hall. Legend has it that prisoners, tried in court, would either be freed on the spot or marched directly to the tree with its handy limbs. Kerby was county seat from 1857 to 1886 when Grants Pass won that honor.

Ominous view of Vulture City hanging tree *(shown opposite)* as seen by prisoners from jail door. 18 of those meeting gruesome death on ironwood tree were usual run of horse thieves and crooked gamblers. One had become enamored of a married woman whose husband was away. Occupied in dalliance, he was surprised by outraged hubby who marched him to tree at gunpoint.

"The Hanging Tree" near Clancey, Montana, is a Ponderosa pine, photo showing (in addition to macabre limb over which rope was thrown) characteristic "plaited" bark texture of this species. (Photo by Jeanne Leeson, Portland school teacher and freelance writer).

GIANT CACTI

Walls of San Miguel Mission, California, are bordered by fine specimens of *Opuntias* of many sorts, ranging from low, slabby prickly pears at left to tree-like chollas, at right.

Fine "grove" of Saguaro cacti *(above)* with Vulture Mountain as backdrop. Site of ghost town of Vulture City is behind photographer and behind scene lies colorful legend. Young Heinrich Heintzel displeased government of his native Austria by digging his own coal and failing to turn it over to authorities. Fleeing his home and kinfolk he surfaced in Arizona with five companions, all searching for gold. Heintzel, changed his name to Wickenburg, was charged with housekeeping duties and wanted to sweep out tent floor. He shot a vulture to get a wing for broom. It fell, thrashing in the dust and Wickenburg, saw glints of gold in sand. This marked the beginnings of one of Arizona's richest mines. Need for horse feed forced growing of hay in nearby Salt River Valley bottom lands and eventual establishment of Phoenix. Photo shows general location of area where Wickenburg shot bird.

Huge "prickly pears" *(above center)* are mute testimonials to some of Luther Burbank's work at his home in Santa Rosa, California. In working with these plants his aim was production of completely spineless ones for cattle feed. Some were quite successful but had tendency to revert to spiny state in time. All forms bear these fruits - deep red and delicious when tiny spines are washed or burned off.

Giant cactus, *(above right) Cereus giganteus*, is well represented in this magnificent specimen growing at edge of ghostly Vulture City, Arizona. Likely it would rate among largest. Height about 35′ to 40′, thickness 1′ to 2′, weight around 5 or 6 tons, plant about 150 years old. Balanced on comparatively small base there would seem to be danger of it being blown over in strong desert winds but cacti rarely fall. Rains are scarce, of short duration and although often heavy, do not soak in deeply. Root system of Saguaro is geared accordingly - very wide - spreading but shallow. "Trunk" has built-in skeleton of heavy, hard rods crowded at base, spreading upwards within limits of heavy "hide". Since Saguaros grow in treeless areas, these straight poles, exposed after death and decay of old plant, called "cardones", are still used by Indians for framework of simple hogans, or other dwellings.

One of nature's stranger quirks is aberrant growth of succulent plants producing such monstrous creations as this Saguaro *(below left)* in garden of San Xavier Del Bac, few miles south of Tucson, Arizona. This one is a most spectacular example of phenomenon distorting plants into weird, almost unrecognizable "monsters". Here however there is also a strange beauty in the unusually symmetrically balanced form.

Donald Culross Peattie, in his *A Natural History of Western Trees*, writes that the holes shown are made by a variety of birds, usually gila woodpecker. These nesting sites are full of sappy water and require a rather long drying period before becoming habitable. In time strong scar tissue is formed, far outlasting the softer parts of dead plant and become usable as containers by Indians.

Growing as base plants here are "Century Plants", *Agave americana*, which while probably originating in Mexico, seem fitting as desert companions to cacti. Old Mission Church is extremely fascinating and much pictured in *Historic Western Churches* by author.

Close-up of Saguaro trunk *(below center).* Although it is known that mice and other desert creatures often inhabit abandoned woodpeckers' nests, question arises - how do the little critters run up and down these spiny paths?

Among ruins of ghostly Madrid, New Mexico, are many remains of stone buildings with earthen roofs *(below)*. Technical definition of "tree" specifies subject be at least 8′ tall. Perhaps these chollas are included here only as a technicality?

Giant Saguaro seen against setting sun. In silhouette fading blooms are seen at tops of branches. These will mature into large fruits, staple in diet of native Indians.

Unique "hedge' of Saguaro cacti at Congress
Junction, Arizona, which appears on maps as
Congress. Originally named Martinez, little
ghost community now, was point of departure
for Congress City that grew up around rich
Congress mine few miles up rough and rocky
road. A handful of people still live at Congress
Junction, attested to by this curious goat.

Flowers of *Yucca filamentosa*, very similar to those of *Y. brevifolia* and far more available for photographing.

Although often popularly termed "cactus", Joshua trees, *Yucca brevifolia*, are in no way related to them. These weird inhabitants of the Southwest desert were supposed to resemble the Biblical figure, Joshua, gesticulating as he prayed to his God. Or, as Mormons have it, pointing out the way to Deseret for the party of Saints established at San Bernardino but summoned back to Salt Lake City by Brigham Young.

The trunks of these strange, ungainly trees are hollow but strong and were once used for surgeons' splints. Also the inner pith was thought to be capable of making good paper and some was fabricated. Fortunately for the Joshua groves, the product was inferior and project was abandoned. Flowers are lily-like and closely related to that family of plants. They are produced abundantly some years and always on terminal spikes (some remnants visible in photo). This tree and young specimens were photographed in Red Rock Canyon, California, on a day so hot the author almost collapsed while absorbed in job.

Old camperdown elm, *Ulmus glabra*, variety camperdown, grows in historic Mountain View Cemetery, Oregon City, Oregon. Among celebrated explorers resting here was Peter Skene Ogden who rescued survivors of Whitman Massacre. Elms in general, except for Chinese ones, are tall, fast growing trees, supreme in parks and large gardens but unsuitable where space is limited, their far-flung roots robbing soil for many feet. Another disadvantage to some elms is ever advancing Dutch elm disease which has decimated their numbers in east and is fast moving to west coast.

Struggle for life ended, twisted remnant of tree stands near summit of Saddle Mountain on western slope of Coast Range near Elsie, Oregon.

Possibly largest in southern Arizona this sycamore, *(above) Platanus Wrightii*, towers over old cemetery at edge of Harshaw ghost town, few miles from Mexican border. This tree and closely related western sycamore in southern California, confines itself to creek beds which offer sub-surface water. One common name, buttonwood, refers to nut-like fruits - little balls strung along slender filament. Tree is known as plane tree in Europe especially where it is used as street tree as in London - that form *P. orientalis*. It is said Plato held his school under a plane tree.

Fraternal order, Woodmen Of The World, once marked graves of deceased members with tombstones resembling tree trunks. This cemetery *(above center)* is at Malheur City, ghost town in eastern Oregon on southern edge of Blue Mountains. Town burned to ground some years ago, flames destroying all wooden structures and headboards in graveyard but sparing these monuments in otherwise treeless area.

Familiar potted "Rubber Plant" *(above)* grows to mature size here in Coronado, California, where it is not injured by frost. Properly *Ficus elastica*, the Indian rubber tree attains huge dimensions in native East Indies.

Weird is the word for this tree. "Dragon Tree",
(above) Dracaena draco, is so called because its
red sap is supposed to be like the blood of a
dragon. Comparatively hardy, enduring light
frosts, it hails from Canary Islands where, it is
reported, specimens may attain an age of 6,000
years (Bailey's Horticultural Encyclopedia).
This "youngster" could well have been planted
at time Hotel Del Coronado was built in early
1880s in Coronado, Califoria.

Pioneer family at home in giant cedar stump
near Edgecomb, Washington, (Notches in
stump were made for springboards when fallers
took tree down). Although not credited here,
photo shows masterful touch of early day
photographer, Darius Kinsey. It was supplied
by Bert Kellog, Port Angeles.

Stump house near Clallam Bay, Washington, was used as studio by early day photographer, P. Wischmeyer. (Photo from Bert Kellog, Port Angeles, Washington).

Elwha, Washington, post office in 1895. Bert Kellog, photographer-historian of Port Angeles, Washington, relates, "In 1895 a U.S. Postal Inspector came to investigate reports that post office in nearby Elwha was housed in an old stump. He found report true and pronounced "structure" a disgrace to the Postal System, ordering that it be rebuilt. Stump was improved to extent shown in this 1900 photo. (Elwha series from Bert Kellog).

This famous Western red cedar stump was 1,000 years and 20′ in diameter when Darius Kinsey found and photographed it near Arlington, Washington. 10 years later it was hollowed out to accommodate road. Pioneer photographer Darius Kinsey drove his Model T through hollowed out cedar stump, posing his wife and son beside it. (Photos from *This Was Logging* by Ralph W. Andrews.)

BIBLIOGRAPHY and ACKNOWLEDGEMENTS

Cone Bearing Trees of Yosemite National Park
Life in California Arthur Robinson, 1891
Lava Cast Forest Fort Rock Ranger District Deschutes
    National Forest
California Missions and Their Romances
    Mrs. Fremont Older
Standard Cyclopedia of Horticulture
    Liberty Hyde Bailey
Trees and Shrubs for Northwest Gardens John A. Grant
Forests of Australia Alexander Rule
East of the Cascades Phil Brogan
A Natural History of Western Trees
    Donald Culross Peattie
Barlow Road Clackamas and Wasco Counties
    Historical Societies
Barlow Road Oregon Historical Society
Beautiful California Lane Publishing Co.
Redwood Classic Ralph W. Andrews
This Was Logging Ralph W. Andrews

The Enduring Giants Joseph Engebreck Jr.
Western States Guides WPA Writers Projects
Genus Pinus N.T. Mirov
Pacific Coast Trees McMinn and Maino
Sharon Nesbit Troutdale Oregon Historical Society
Archie Satterfield Seattle *Post-Intelligencer*
Ann Sullivan *The Oregonian* (Portland)
Mrs. A.T. Hibbard Helena, Montana
William Calvin Robinson Foreman, Portland, Oregon,
    City Parks System
Casey Kendall Portland, Oregon
Gladstone, Oregon, Public Library
Multnomah County Public Library Portland, Oregon
Joe Stalheim Oroville, Washington
Richard Rickman Portland, Oregon
Raymond House Portland, Oregon
Milwaukie Historical Society Milwaukie, Oregon
Mrs. William D. McDonald Milwaukie, Oregon

INDEX